LEFT BEHIND AND LOVING IT

Left Behind &
Loving It

A Cheeky Look at the End Times

D. MARK DAVIS

CASCADE *Books* · Eugene, Oregon

LEFT BEHIND AND LOVING IT
A Cheeky Look at the End Times

Cascade Books
An Imprint of Wipf and Stock Publishers
199 W. 8th Ave., Suite 3
Eugene, OR 97401

www.wipfandstock.com

ISBN 13: 978-1-60899-826-5

Cataloging-in-Publication data:

Davis, D. Mark

Left behind and loving it : a cheeky look at the end times / D. Mark Davis

xii + 118 p. ; 23 cm. Includes bibliographical references.

ISBN 13: 978-1-60899-826-5

1. End of the world. 2. Rapture (Christian eschatology). 3. Apocalyptic literature—History and criticism. I. Title.

BS646 D3 2011

Manufactured in the U.S.A.

To Chris, for constant encouragement and support,
from the plane ride that sparked the idea of writing this book
to the wild ride of putting it together.

Contents

Preface

A FEW YEARS AGO, I received in the mail a foldout, full-color brochure that was all about hidden prophecies in the Bible regarding Iraq, Iran, and America. It was filled with the typical stuff of Left Behind Theology paraphernalia—references to Daniel's cryptic writings, as well as explanations of how the "New World Order" and "War on Terrorism" are the present-day meanings of those cryptic writings. But, there was one feature to this brochure that I found very surprising.

The brochure was full of photographs of very recognizable people: George W. Bush, Saddam Hussein, Osama bin Laden, Vladimir Putin, Yasser Arafat, Mohammed Khatami, and even Tony Blair. It had small maps showing Iran and Iraq, Estonia, Latvia, and Lithuania, as well as the "Asian Tigers." It had the U.S. presidential seal and the flags of Israel, Great Britain, the U.S., and Russia. It had a Star of David affixed into the title. And after all of these very obvious, very recognizable pictures of actual people and countries, there was a statement at the bottom that read, "The views expressed here . . . are not intended to represent, favorably or unfavorably, any person, persons, national or ethnic group."

Good grief. There's nothing uglier than passive-aggressive prophesying. I just cannot imagine John the Baptizer saying, "And finally, when I began this sermon with the words, 'You brood of vipers!' please understand that I was not intending anything favorable or unfavorable by it."

I think prophecy in the twenty-first century is having an identity crisis. We seem to think that prophetic texts in the Bible are the predictive forecasts of wild-eyed people who didn't bathe properly, but saw the future with astounding clarity. And, we seem to think that we have the task of figuring out what they meant by all of their symbolic language, so that just before all of the predicted calamities come down on the world, we can be rescued by the "rapture" and will not be "left behind" to suffer through it.

For reasons biblical and theological, I think we are wrong on both counts. This book is an attempt to explain why and to offer some better ways of reading scary apocalyptic texts from the Bible.

Acknowledgments

FROM MY OWN CHILDHOOD as part of a tradition that espouses Left Behind Theology, to my current work as a pastor in the Presbyterian Church (USA), this book reflects the passion, insights, and support that I have received from many different directions in my own faith journey. I especially thank Douglas Beacham, who encouraged me in my first year of college to allow my head to speak as loudly as my heart. He may regret that now. Douglas F. Ottati encouraged me in seminary to allow my heart to speak as loudly as my head. It is amazing how two Dougs, saying opposite things, both said the right thing to me in ways that I will always appreciate. I also owe special thanks to J. Kenneth Kuntz, who kindly read portions of chapter 2, fixing the wrong things and chuckling at the right things. I needed that.

Most of all, I owe thanks to the many voices that have accompanied me on the swirling paths of my faith journey. You know who you are. I do not hold you responsible for what follows, only for the joy of the journey. Thanks.

Introduction

Left Behind and Hating It

ANYONE WHO LOOKS THROUGH the religion section of a bookstore or watches religious programming on television might assume that the only Christian view of the end of the world is a kind of "rapture–tribulation–second coming" scenario with the primary concern of whether one will be taken away in the "rapture" or be "left behind" to suffer the consequences. That assumption is simply not true. In fact, throughout the history of the church there have been many different ways of understanding what the Scriptures have to say about the end of the world, beginning with what the phrase "the end of the world" even means. Books like Tim LaHaye's and Jerry B. Jenkins's Left Behind series, as well as numerous radio and television expressions of Christianity, offer what looks like a clear explanation of what the end of the world will look like. I call those kinds of explanations "Left Behind Theology," and this book is a way of calling them into question.

What Is Left Behind Theology?

The basic idea of Left Behind Theology is something like this: Jesus is coming again and this time he is bringing some attitude. It reminds me of that great line from the movie "Tombstone," with Wyatt Earp—played by Kurt Russell sporting one righteous-looking handlebar mustache. Wyatt is shuffling out of town because his enemies have humiliated him, shot his best friend, and are forcing him to get on a train heading east. While these experiences put him in a perfect position to go back east and become an awesome country music songwriter, instead Wyatt Earp pulls himself together, shoots his escorts, killing all but one of them, and sends that one back, wounded, with a message that he screams through the driving rain: "Tell them I'm coming back, and hell's coming with me!"

Naturally, at first I thought this meant that Goldie Hawn was going to come back with him and give those bad guys a really strong pouty look, but, no, it meant that Wyatt and his crew were coming back to defeat the bad guys' violence with a greater good-guy violence. "Typical Hollywood," you might think, but the roots of "good-guy violence" go way back before Tinseltown was ever established.

This is the kind of Jesus that Left Behind Theology says is coming again. This Jesus says, "You didn't like me as the 'meek and mild' Jesus in my first visit to earth, eh? Couldn't wait to get rid of me, eh? Thought that cross would be the end of it, huh? Well, just remember that I'm coming back and hell's coming with me!" (It helps if you imagine driving rain, a tattered hat, and that way cool Kurt Russell handlebar mustache on top of Jesus' customary white robe and beard.) It almost makes you wonder why anyone in the early church thought it was a good idea to pray, "Come Lord Jesus!" They might as well have added "and bring hell with you next time!"

But, of course, the scenario of Left Behind Theology is a bit more involved than a two-hour movie. After all, how can there be an entire industry and a multi-volume thriller series based on a thin plot like "Jesus: Mad"? In fact, within the plot of Left Behind Theology, Jesus' mad dash back to the scene of the crime is preceded by a lot of other stuff. It can get as convoluted as the War of Roses, but it looks something like this:

1) *Before* Jesus comes back breathing fire he is going to sneak in "like a thief in the night" in order to take some of us away first. This particular sneaky return is not really the "Second Coming" *per se*. And, of course, it's not the "First Coming," which happened two thousand years ago. It's more like the "First and a Half Coming." In fact, in Left Behind Theology, Jesus doesn't even make it all the way down to earth. He stops in the sky for a nanosecond and good Christians meet him up there, when they all return swiftly to heaven. The First and a Half Coming is typically called the "rapture." So, Christians are raptured and get to watch the rest of this scenario from the nose-

bleed section—except for all of the filthy hypocrites, who get a much closer seat.

"Is Jesus coming again then?," you ask. Oh no, not for a while yet.

2) Jesus is not coming until *after* these four creepy horse riders plague the earth, each horse a different color and each color representing a different kind of widespread massacre sent straight from God. We will see that Jesus' coming gets delayed a lot because Jesus is very polite and always deferring to others. Unfortunately, those "others" tend to wreak a lot of havoc. "Is Jesus coming then?," you ask.

3) The answer is, "Hold your four horses." Jesus will not come again until *after* the arrival of an imposter who is named "Antichrist" but called other stuff for a while first. This awful person has a pet beast (unimaginatively called the "Beast") that kills a lot of people, invents barcoding to impress his secret number on the doomed, and then starts a major mother-of-all-wars to kill a lot more people so that the only people left are those poor souls who beg rocks to kindly fall on top of them and get them out of this mess. The mess is called the "tribulation," and it involves lots and lots of blood.

Is Jesus coming then? Not yet.

4) We still have to let an angel put up with the Beast for a while and then kill it and throw it into a deep, deep, deep pit. Just be glad we don't have to wait for the "kerplunk" at the bottom of the pit because we would be waiting forever and ever. It is a *bottomless* pit.

Is Jesus coming then? Almost, but not quite yet.

5) The imposter, who has dropped the pretentions and is going by his real name "Antichrist" now—finally gets whacked, more people die, and this gal called the "Great Whore of Babylon" loses her looks, develops a drinking problem, and goes out of business because all of her customers turn on her. Oh, and she has these two twin brothers named Gog and Magog, who show up and promptly get killed.

Now, is Jesus coming? Yes!

6) Finally, Jesus comes! And when Jesus comes the seven people that are left alive on the earth will be saved and get to go to heaven and

spend eternity with the people who got raptured up there in the first place. (I think they should have to wipe up all of that blood first, but that's just me.)

The moral of this story is that you want to be the kind of Christian that gets taken up in the "rapture" in the first place! How do you do that? Well, you have to purchase the right kind of study Bible that comes with a complete set of highlighter pens and a seventy-five-page timeline that gives a day-by-day description of this chaos. The best part of this scenario, however, is that those who are raptured in the first place get to spend the rest of eternity saying, "I told you so!" to those seven people who had to endure the entire tribulation. Now that sounds like fun in a nice, clean, heavenly sort of way.

Left Behind Theology and the History of the Church

As you can see, underneath all of the bizarre characters that come and go, Left Behind Theology is built around a fairly Hollywood-predictable plot-line with lots of action, buckets of blood, some tension-filled moments, and that same old twist that the whipped puppy will come back and settle things just when the bad guys least expect it. It is no wonder, then, that the early church simply bypassed the details by using shorthand saying, "Come, Lord Jesus." We know exactly what they meant by that.

Or do we? The problem with the straightforwardness of this plotline is that most of the faithful people throughout the history of Christianity would have looked at this scenario and said, "What the . . . ?" If they were biblically literate—and, of course, very few people were biblically literate before the invention of highlighter pens—they might have recognized some of the biblical allusions within the scenario. That's easy enough. However, the whole idea that this drama is going to unfold in such a literal way would be strange indeed. Even worse, the idea that someone in our day would put all of the disparate pieces of the puzzle together with such certainty would be troubling. But worst of all, the assumption that this scenario would magnificently affirm all of our presuppositions and even our political loyalties—as Left Behind Theology is often is construed to do—would be downright heretical. Our predecessors might have even accused us of using the word of God to fit our own agendas—the very thing prohibited by the fourth commandment, "Do not take God's name in vain."

While the historic church has had many different ideas about what the "end of the world" might look like, it has consistently remembered one thing: time and eternity are in God's hands, not ours. Even Jesus responded to questions about the timing of the end times by saying, "I don't know," because the comprehension of time and eternity belongs to God and God alone. Therefore, any time we talk about the end of the world we should remember that everything we are saying makes some claim about God. If we believe in the long-standing claim that God is the creator and sustainer of the world, then what we have to say about the end of the world really matters. If we say, for example, "God is going to get angry one day and smoke the world like a fine cigar," then we are making the claim that God's love for the world is unreliable. If we say, "One day all the really good people will disappear from the earth and the rest of humanity is going to get tortured for a long time," then we are still saying something about God, even if we don't use God's name. The point is, our talk about the end of the world is always, at the same time, talk about God, God's way, and God's care for the world.

It is almost impossible not to wonder and talk about the end of the world—especially now that we know how truly small our earth is in the larger scheme of things and how fragile it is. In fact, in some ways we definitely *should* be talking about the "end of the world." But, when we do so, we should remember that the things we say about the end of the world are claims about God. That means that we are doing theology. And one of the greatest temptations for anyone doing theology is the temptation to project agendas onto God. Likewise, when we read the Scriptures and try to say what they mean about the "end of the world," we are interpreting. That means that we are making critical judgments about meaning. The great temptation here is to be presumptuous and imagine that our opinion about what Scripture means is the same as The Truth.

Left Behind Theology makes a lot of claims about the "end of the world" and about what the Scriptures mean. It particularly relies on being able to "break the code" and to tell us what symbols in the Bible really mean. Again, the church throughout history was a lot more cautious. Even when historical events seemed closely similar to some biblical symbolism, the historic church usually (not always, but usually) remembered that symbolic language can often represent more than just one thing. So, using biblical symbols to understand historical events and offer comfort, correction, or encouragement is one thing. To presume that we can *prove* anything by aligning biblical symbols with events of our day is another thing. All symbols, imagery, and stories of the Bible are part of an unfolding cosmology that has been a "God story" all the way back to the words, "When God began creating the heavens and the earth . . ."

So, consider how someone like Martin Luther might react to Left Behind Theology.[1] He would be aghast at so many levels. For Luther, the "Antichrist" was clearly the Roman Catholic Pope and the "Beast" was a Turk. But Lutherans today do not make Luther's interpretation of these terms into their doctrine of the end times. I'm sure there are some weird, mean-spirited bloggers among us today who are still banging on the "pope = Antichrist" drum, but by and large most Lutherans today would happily share a cream puff with a Catholic friend and call it a good time. And I don't know anyone today who is still afraid of the big bad Turk, do you?

Personally, I think Luther was way off on this pope and Turk thing. But at least he was not saying it like this: "Yeah, we Protestants get to disappear, then this pope pretends to be a nice guy for three and a half years, but then he'll show his true colors for the next three and a half years before he gets whacked, and then we Protestants get to come back and have a thousand years of peace." And it's a good thing that Luther did not get that specific, because here we are five hundred years later with Catholics and Lutherans eating cream puffs together!

My guess is that five hundred years from now people will roll their eyes at the casual confidence behind the predictions in Left Behind Theology. They might say things like, "Can you imagine that someone once thought the European Union would be the beginning of 'one world government'? Ha! They couldn't even agree on a currency!" And won't we look silly when they say that? That's why we just should step back a few steps before we buy into this whole business of Left Behind Theology that

1. Martin Luther is the sixteenth century German theologian whose protests against and attempts at reforming the church of his day led to what was later called the Protestant Reformation. While he is often confused with Martin Luther King, Jr., the twentieth century African American theologian and social reformer who advocated for civil rights, they are not the same person. They are not even cousins. They are, however, both in my 'top ten' list of favorite people in history.

seems to have all the puzzle pieces put together into one single best-selling scenario.

The Real Questions underlying Left Behind Theology

It is not that I think Tim LaHaye is just making wrong guesses when he writes all of his Left Behind novels or when he expounds on the end of the world in his non-fictional books. I think the whole business of trying to make one-to-one connections between the symbols in the biblical story and various events in our own day is suspect. And we should especially be concerned if the scenarios end up painting God as a scary ogre, Jesus as a vengeful gunslinger, and people we don't like as the arch-nemesis of God and the holy angels. Nonetheless, underlying the misbegotten scenarios of Left Behind Theology are some real questions that deserve our attention:

- How *do* we read weird "apocalyptic" biblical texts faithfully? And, let's be honest, there are plenty of weird "apocalyptic" biblical texts. With all of their grotesque and over-the-top symbolism, aren't they supposed to scare the snot out of us?

- If Jesus got murdered when he was a meek and mild servant-type, why wouldn't he reinvent himself and come back a little more buff with a lot more edge? It worked for Kurt Russell!

- Aren't our enemies God's enemies too? After all, we have "In God We Trust" on our coins. What do they have? Pictures of old Turks!

- And, finally, isn't God kind of mean anyway? Really, what would prevent God from raining havoc down on us like God did to others back in the good old days?

The truth is, I think these are legitimate questions that deserve some well-reasoned and thoughtful answers. I hope you find some one day, but until then, please allow me to take a few whacks at them in this book. To do so, however, I think it is important for us to begin with the most often-repeated statement in all of the Scriptures as our absolute starting point. Do you know what that is? It's this: "God's steadfast love endures forever." I tried to count the number of times that this statement is in the Scriptures and had to quit because there was one psalm that used up all of my fingers and toes twice. In just one psalm! (Psalm 136 for all of you doubt-filled fact-checkers.) By the time I quit trying to count every time that phrase appears in the Scriptures, I had no doubt whatsoever that God's steadfast love is the absolute starting point of any way of speaking about God, if you care about things like biblical integrity. So, even though we have real anxieties about the future, even though some of these questions that I've identified are truly compelling questions, and even though some things that transpire in life seem eerily poignant in some big-picture way, our starting point must always be, "God's steadfast love endures forever."

No, Not That Rapture, the Next One; No, Wait the Next One; No, . . .

It is because God's steadfast love endures forever that I reject the entire premise of Left Behind Theology—that the only way to survive the future is to be swept away from this world while God and Satan duke it out for supremacy. In fact, if Left Behind Theology adherents truly believed their own reports, the "rapture" would have taken place several times before now. Here are just a few of the signal events from the fairly recent past that people were just absolutely sure would be the moment when the "rapture" takes place:

- 1948, when Israel was re-established as a sovereign nation again—that was the mother lode of possibilities for the "rapture." Didn't happen.

- 1978, when Israel and Egypt signed the Camp David Peace Accords, I had a friend who left off watching the signatures on television to go pray in his dorm room because his pastor had shown him—from the Bible!—that Jesus would come to rapture the saints at that exact moment. Didn't happen. Well, it *almost* happened when one of the guys in our dorm took his shoes off and sneaked out of the room while the rest of us started pointing and saying, "Steve look, Todd is gone!" But, even then, it didn't *really* happen.

- 1984, when Ronald (six letters) Wilson (six letters) Reagan (six letters!) was three and a half years into his unlikely ascendancy to the presidential throne, would have been a great time for the "rapture" to take place. As you may have heard, 666 is supposed to be the secret number called the "mark of the Beast," which truly damns anyone who is "left behind" for eternity. But Ronald Wilson Reagan eventually gave way to George Herbert Walker Bush, whose name just doesn't add up biblically at all, unless the Reagan-Bush years were supposed to give us the Beast's secret *phone* number. (It would be 666-6764, but you may need to dial 1 and the area code first.) So, even President 666 was not the true harbinger of the "rapture."

- And I haven't even mentioned the celestial events that were supposed to usher in the "rapture," such as the planets being aligned, Halley's Comet, the sun hiding behind a total eclipse, Pluto losing its "planet" status, Halley's Comet again, or the calendar flipping over from 1999 to 2000 and causing all kinds of "Y2K" havoc.

Since none of those scary dates and celestial movements in fact ended the world (not from the view of my window, anyway), there is only one logical course for humanity to follow: Make up a new "end of the world" date. After all, if we lose the "rapture card," we lose one of the most effective evangelism tools Christianity ever invented. So, imagine this: In the year 2012, when the writers of *The Office* have finally run out of script ideas; when baby boomers are all collecting Social Security and cashing in their U.S. Savings Bonds *at the same time*; when the Chicago Cubs actually win the World Series; and when the spirits of the ancient Mayans rise from their graves and lead the long-gone Mayan civilization to victory in the Summer Olympics—wouldn't that be just the right time for the "rapture" to come?

See how a part of you wants to say "That's ridiculous!" but another part is afraid that if you say it you might miss out on the "rapture"? See how you fear having to suffer through boring television, a collapsed financial market, incorrigible Chicago natives, and listening to the Mayan national anthem over and over again?[2] That's the kind of ongoing anxiety that Left Behind Theology evokes. And it seems entirely contrary to the kind of comfort that comes in the words, "God's steadfast love endures forever."

2. The Ancient Mayan national anthem is twenty-six minutes long and consists of only three notes, two of which are dissonant. It's very hard to listen to once, much less over and over again during the Olympics. Riots and chaotic discord would surely follow.

The bottom line is this: If Left Behind Theology had been correct in the past, then the "rapture" has probably already taken place and those of us reading this book are already "left behind." If the next best guess is correct, then the "rapture" will take place quite soon and those who are left behind will undoubtedly be forced to read this book as part of the tribulation. In either case, I suggest that we put our faith in that repetitive phrase and simply trust that, left behind or not, God's steadfast love endures forever.

What This Book Is Up To

This book is addressed to three groups of people in particular. First, to those who have been raised within the belief system of Left Behind Theology, like I have, this book is an invitation to reconsider this view of the end times biblically and theologically. I am assuming that the people who write and preach Left Behind Theology do so seriously and sincerely. I want to respectfully argue that the biblical interpretations of Left Behind Theology are seriously flawed and the theological claims of Left Behind Theology are sincerely wrong.

Second, to those critics of the Christian faith, who assume that Left Behind Theology is the predominant view of the Christian church, I want to argue otherwise. I understand how Left Behind Theology seems to depict the Christian church as an escapist religion and seems to imply that the Christian church has no stake in the ongoing sustainability of the earth. I hope to show that, in fact, many of the Scriptures that are used to shape Left Behind Theology are about radical engagement in the world, not an escape from it. And while this book is not about environmental matters *per se*, I at least want to show that the kind of irresponsibility that many persons exhibit toward the fate of the earth in the name of Left Behind Theology is not the best Christian alternative.

Third, I want to appeal to those persons within the Christian church who do not accept Left Behind Theology, but who do not know how else to read scary apocalyptic biblical texts. I fear that too many people of faith cannot wrap their own hearts around Left Behind Theology, but assume that they are being non-biblical when they admit that. And many pulpits contribute to the confusion by simply ignoring these texts altogether. The truth is, those scary apocalyptic texts are saying things that are terribly important. This book offers one way of taking those important texts seriously.

We'll begin with trying to develop an appreciation for the Scripture's use of poetic language as a way of expressing depth and meaning. Most of the apocalyptic texts in the New Testament—those texts where Left Behind Theology gets its mojo—are written poetically, so it's important to begin there. Then, we'll look at Daniel, the wellspring of most of Left Behind Theology's approach to the Scriptures. I agree that Daniel is a key book to embrace when trying to interpret many of the apocalyptic texts in the New Testament. So, from Daniel we'll move to the Gospels, particularly Mark, Luke, and Matthew—in that order, for reasons that I will explain. These New Testament writers very self-consciously make use of Daniel when telling their story of Jesus. Finally, we'll look at that enigmatic book of Revelation, which seems so intimidating to many people of faith. I will not try to explain everything that we encounter in these apocalyptic texts. What I want to offer in this book are some reading strategies for taking these texts seriously, even if we do not take them literally.

It is my hope that you enjoy reading this book as much as I've enjoyed writing it. But remember, even as we explore serious apocalyptic texts, we should never forget that God's steadfast love endures forever. Because of that, we can speak of the future, the unknown, the inscrutable, and even prediction about the supposedly imminent "rapture" with a tone of joy and confidence, knowing that nothing is able to separate us from the love of God. Therefore, we do not live with the anxiety of being "left behind." Let the prognostications come and go. If "left behind" is how God rolls, then in the name of God's steadfast love we can be left behind and loving it.

1

Ascension Deficit Disorder

The Art of Reading Poetically

The Mysterious Case of the Missing Rapture

LEFT BEHIND THEOLOGY GIVES the impression that there are numerous places in the Bible that read something like this:

> *"And on that day," says the Lord of Hosts, "I will send forth my chosen one to smite the earth. And yea shall my chosen one first rapture the blessed away from the face of the earth, after which I will pour out my wrath upon all evildoers and many signs and wonders shall break forth. There shall be much weeping and gnashing of teeth over the course of seven years and then shall there cometh a time of peace, as it appeareth on the enclosed timeline. Verily." (Zedediah 3:16).*

There are two problems with this pseudo-text from Zedediah 3:16 that I'd like to point out. The first is that there is no book of Zedediah in the Bible. I made that part up. But, if I have another son I'm going to suggest Zedediah to my wife as a pretty cool name. "Yo, Zed, want a cookie?" That has a nice flow to it. Heck, I might even suggest it if we have another daughter. I think for a daughter one ought to leave off the "h."

The second problem with this pseudo-text from Zedediah is that if it were in the Bible, it would be the *only* place where the word "rapture" occurs. That's right, there is no mention of the word "rapture" anywhere in the Bible. That's a troubling fact, since the word "rapture" plays such a significant role in Left Behind Theology. A *very* significant role. Significant as in "the next great event on the timeline of the history of the world." In Left Behind Theology, "rapture" refers to that instantaneous moment when Jesus sneaks in like a thief in the night and snatches all of the true Christians out of this world, just prior to the onset of awful events known as the "tribulation."[1] Now, linear thinkers might look at the fact that the word "rapture" is not actually in the Bible and jump to the conclusion that the whole business of the rapture is not really biblical after all. I felt that way myself, until I ran across this excellent piece of scholarship and reasoning on a blog called, "You Can Look Forward to a Hole in the Ground, I'm Looking Forward to a Hole in the Sky," by Dr. Calamity Endall. Here is an excerpt from the Q&A portion of the blog that really seems to settle the whole issue regarding the case of the missing rapture.

> *Dear Dr. Endall,*
>
> *I am at my wit's end! I know that the rapture is the most important doctrine in the Bible and that everything we do, every single day we live, and every single decision we make is driven by knowing that any second the rapture could happen and only those who are watching and ready will go in it. I know that is true because I have read every book on the subject and I know that God would never want one of his truly loved ones to go through the kind of terrible ordeals that are going to take place during the latter half of the seven years of Tribulation. And, I listen to your radio show faithfully every day to understand exactly where we are on God's great end-time calendar.*
>
> *But, I just cannot seem to find the definitive proof of the rapture in my Bible! My friends—especially those nominal Christian friends of mine—keep challenging me to show them where the doctrine is clearly given, but I cannot even find the word "rapture" in there. I've consulted all of my study Bibles, even Strong's exhaustive concordance, and especially my grandmother's Scofield Reference Bible, but I can't find the word "rapture"! I don't want any more explanations and complicated charts. I just want to be able to point*

---

1. This is the sequence for the "pre-tribulation" rapture. In the "post-tribulation" view, seven years of awful events occur prior to the rapture. The "post-trib" scenario doesn't have the same kind of sudden sneakiness to it to warrant a "thief in the night" description. Anyone can count to seven.

to the word and show my friends that they, too, must be ready! Can
you please help me?
– Need it in Black and White

Dear NiBaW,

Thank you for your letter and your faithfulness amongst this evil
and doomed generation. And thank you for your contributions to
our radio program. My wife Ladeen and I remember you kindly in
our prayers each and every day.

Now, concerning your question of the word "rapture," I am
going to "shew you a mystery" that even the most respected scholars
of our day cannot begin to fathom. You are absolutely correct to say
that the rapture is THE most important doctrine in the entire Bible.
But, you are also correct to say that you cannot find it in your
Bible, or in any Bible known to man. Now, why is that?

Do not be led astray by those doubters and skeptics who say
that the word is not in the Bible because it is not a biblical word!
As we have already shown, it is the most important doctrine "in the
Bible." Just look around you and you will see that it is only the truly
"Bible believing" churches in our world who uphold this teaching
that came straight from the mouth of Jesus. But, here is the reason
you cannot find it:

The word "rapture" has been raptured.

Just think about it. We KNOW that it was there—probably in
many, many places throughout the Old and New Testaments—but,
suddenly, it is no longer there! It is as if two men were working in
the field when, suddenly, one is taken and the other left! It is proof
amazing that, of all the words in the Bible, this is the only one
that is not there any more. That is what some scholars call a "self-
instantiating" word. The word "rapture," in order to demonstrate
beyond any doubt that it is true, has been taken away from us—
gone without a trace, just like you and I will be if we hold firmly to
this word, even when it is not there.

Now, this is a deep teaching and many of your friends will
scoff at it. But, do not be dismayed or led astray by them, for the
wisdom of this world is foolishness to those of us who understand
these great mysteries.

Thank you again for your letter. Please find the enclosed, addressed envelope for your contribution as we continue to spread the
word to our lost and forsaken world.

Yours Truly,
Dr. Endall

Well, there you go. I guess it was silly of me to assume that since the word "rapture" is not in the Scriptures that, perhaps, it is not a biblical word. Nonetheless, I have to say—with all due respect to Dr. Endall—that if the "rapture" is such a pivotal moment in history, then God should have left behind at least one mention of the word "rapture" in the Scriptures in order to offer salvation to those of us who are daft enough to want our theology thoroughly grounded in the (existing) Word of God. So, since the word "rapture" is not (currently) a biblical word, it is my intention to put the word "rapture" in quotation marks for the rest of my life. When you see the word "rapture," it is my shorthand for "that so-called 'rapture' that Dr. Endall claims is biblical."

So, to be clear, when Left Behind Theology talks about the "rapture," here is what is intended: At some unexpected moment—which could be any time now because all of the preparatory stuff leading up to this moment has been fulfilled at least once—Jesus will sneak back to earth like "a thief in the night" and snatch away all of the true Christians. They will rise upward, suddenly, into heaven in a manner very much like the ascension of Jesus that Luke describes at the end of his Gospel (Luke 24:50–53) and, again, at the beginning of the book of Acts (Acts 1:9–11). When Luke describes the ascension, he speaks about the disciples watching Jesus being lifted up until "a cloud received him out of their sight." The "rapture" seems modeled on Jesus' ascension, but at 800x fast-forward speed, described as "in the twinkling of an eye." That is why, in both serious and comical pictorial representations of this event, artists show nothing but ankles and feet still sticking out of the bottom of the clouds—those people zipped up quickly!

So, that's the "rapture" that we hear so much about in Left Behind Theology. And it is the suddenness of the event that makes it so . . . threatening. The "evangelistic" twist of this scenario goes like this: "Sooner or later, God's patience is done, we're outta here, and you blew it. Big mistake. I wish we'd all been ready, but you weren't and now you have to suffer the consequences." One could almost write the beginning of a multi-volume thriller about the immediate catastrophes of the rapture: large jetliners suddenly being pilot-less; military brigades all weaponed up with nobody there to lead them; or cashiers at Starbucks drive-through windows suddenly not responding through the speaker to our orders anymore. And one longer-termed catastrophe could unfold over the rest of the series:

All of the evil governments of the world will seize the moment to wreak havoc. Of course, every evil government has a secret manual hidden underneath their nuclear button that reads, *How to Start the Tribulation Once All of Those Pesky Real Christians Are Gone*. And they will. So Left Behind evangelism says, "You had better sign up for the rapture now, because you don't want to be around to see what happens later!"

The Scriptures' Poetic Language

As you can tell from my tone of writing, I am not persuaded that the "rapture" or this particular end-time scenario is really part of the Christian message. I do admit, however, that the Bible often does make some pretty bold, sometimes scary, often threatening statements about what is called the "day of the Lord." The meaning of those statements is often hard to grasp. One reason is because the Scriptures' preferred language for communicating God's intentions—both threats and blessings—is poetic language. And poetic language works differently than the kind of precise language that one might rightly expect in a scientific textbook, a treatise on history, or an end-of-the-world timeline. Allow me to illustrate.

Lover looks Beloved in the eyes and says, "I want to kiss you with a thousand kisses." A thousand kisses! What a beautiful expression of love, passion, and foreplay! Of course Beloved is going to look back into Lover's eyes and say, "Have at it, Baby!" But, I suggest that Lover and Beloved, no matter how deep the love or mad the passion, will not "have at it"—at least, not if "having at it" means actually kissing a thousand times. I'll bet they don't get much past thirty, or fifty if they are younger than sixteen—unless one of them is wearing braces, then we're back to thirty. Why? Because my college education tells me that, after about fifteen or twenty kisses, you are basically making out with your own saliva. After twenty it's disgusting and after thirty you are a *bona fide* nut case to keep going. Mae West was simply wrong when she said that too much of a good thing is wonderful. Not when it involves spit.

So, questions: 1) Was Lover lying? 2) Was Lover caught up in the heat of the moment and just trying to score? 3) Was Lover just really bad at math? The answers are: 1) no, 2) not necessarily (although one can't rule it out entirely), and 3) not that I know of. But the primary reason that Lover spoke of a thousand kisses even though that's not what he actually meant is because Lover was speaking *poetically*. And when one speaks poetically, one uses hyperbole, exaggeration, and expressions like "passion that could melt an iceberg" in order to express the depth of one's love. What we do not do when expressing depth is speak literally! That would be really bad karma. Just imagine if Lover had said, "I want to kiss you about eight times, one of them really long, and then talk for a few moments while we dry out a bit, then kiss a little more, then . . ." I can tell you that Lover would be talking to himself before too long.

Poetic language is how we try to express depth, whether it is a deep sense of love, hate, anger, vengeance, wonder, violation, horror, or sorrow. It is what we mumble at funerals, shout at rallies, whisper when stargazing, and giggle at parties. It is only a small, small part of poetic language that worries about rhyming, iambic pentameters, or symmetry. The point of poetry is not to explain, argue, or to be precise; it is to express. Poetic speaking is that moment when your heart finds an artistic voice. And that is what Lover is all about when longing to kiss Beloved a thousand times. So, the correct response for us is not to say, "Eww, that's gross!" but "Aww, that's sweet."

It is a huge problem to take poetic speech literally. It almost guarantees misunderstanding. That is one of the reasons there are such deep misunderstandings between Western nations and Middle Eastern nations, where poetic speech is still used frequently. So, some leader from the Middle East will use a phrase that is ridiculous when taken literally, like "This will be the mother of all wars." We know that it will not be the mother of all wars, partly because wars don't have babies, but mainly because he is not speaking literally. Nonetheless Western cartoonists, late-night comedians, and that guy at the barber shop who never actually gets his hair cut will have a field day making jokes out of it. And it *is* kind of funny, but mostly in an "I don't really understand what I'm talking about" sort of way. The laughing stops, however, when pundits, wonks, elected officials, and other such cultural ruffians begin to treat this poetic language as if it were literal and to respond with something other than jokes.

The same problem can happen when we read the Bible, which was written by folks who thought that just about all religious expression was worthy of poetic speech. Let's look at a couple of examples of well-known biblical stories that show how poetic speech works differently from literal speech.

17

Exhibit A: Creation Stories

The first creation story in the Bible is a beautiful expression of God's loving initiative in creating every aspect of the world from shining stars to creeping vermin, piece by piece, over six movements called "days." After the world is created and declared "good," God takes a Sabbath.[2] When we read it as poetry, this story says so much about the dignity and beauty of life, about how every element of creation is derived from the very word of God, and how all of creation moves toward Sabbath rest with God. However, if we read this story literally, we transmogrify it into an astronomical or geological or biological discourse that causes school boards to disclaim the existence of Tyrannosaurus Rex.

Or, think about the second creation story, where God is no longer speaking creation into existence, but getting down and dirty with the dust of the earth in forming creation.[3] First, God makes Adam, then animals—none of which are suitable mates for Adam—all out of dirt. This story was originally written in Hebrew, where the wordplay between "ground" (*Adamah*) and the first human (*Adam*) is unmistakable. That is why biblical scholar Bill Brown calls this human the "groundling."[4] Then, something wonderful happens to this molded lump of dirt: "the LORD God formed *adam* from the dust of the ground, and breathed into his nostrils the breath of life; and the *adam* became a living being" (Genesis 2:7).

Not only is the relationship between *adamah* and *adam* important in this telling of creation, so is the fact that the word for "breath" is the same word in Hebrew for "spirit." So, when God "breathes" (inspirits) the "breath" (spirit) into *adam*, we think of breathing and we think of the animating spirit that marks the difference between molded clay and a living being. When a story is told with two words that have systemic connections—like "groundling" and "ground"—and another word has multiple meanings—like "breath" and "spirit"—we can be pretty sure that we're in

2. The "first creation story" refers to Genesis 1:1—2:4a. I'm sorry for the awkward numbers, but a long time ago, whoever initially added chapter and verse divisions to the Scriptures really missed the mark on where this one actually ends. This story is typically called the "first" creation story because of the order of appearance in the Scriptures. It is probably not the oldest creation story in the Bible. But, I digress.

3. The "second creation story" refers to Genesis 2:4b–3:24, which includes what is often called the "fall" of Adam and Eve and their expulsion from the garden.

4. Brown, *The Seven Pillars of Creation*, 80–81.

the territory of poetic language. Part of the power of poetry is that the words point beyond any kind of simple one-to-one relationship to what they are describing. Even in the bad poetry of homemade Valentine's Day cards, words like "madness" can take on the meaning of a deep, deep passion, rather than just "crazier than a bean on a rose bush."

If we took them literally, the two creation stories at the beginning of the book of Genesis would cause problems. Some of the details of the two stories are simply irreconcilable. For example, the first story has animals being created prior to humans and, when humans are created, man and woman are created at the same time, so that together they embody the "image of God." The second story has Adam being created first, then animals, then Eve out of Adam's rib. If the stories were intended to be taken literally as geology or anthropology, those differences would pose a problem. Literalists who want to defend the Bible look for ways to reconcile the differences; literalists who want to dismiss the Bible point to the differences as their "proof" that the Bible is wrong. But, the problem does not lie in the Bible; the problem lies in trying to read poetic texts literally.

Exhibit B: The Flood Story

Let's look at one more example of the problem of reading poetic texts literally, before turning to one of the primary texts that is very popular with Left Behind Theology. This example is a problem that arises for every child who has ever gone through Sunday School and has taken what they've heard seriously. And it has to do with one of the most well-known stories of the Bible, that comic-tragic story of Noah's ark (Genesis 6–9).

Small children often see the story of Noah's ark as a comedy—not in the sense of being funny, but in the sense that, in the end, "all's well that ends well." This way of viewing the story is why children in Sunday School love to take home pictures of two giraffes, two elephants, and two monkeys climbing aboard a wooden boat. Peter Spier's book *Noah's Ark* is a fetching example of seeing this story as a comedy. On the other hand, when these same Sunday School children get older, they begin to revisit this story with a measure of horror. They are no longer looking at the smiling faces of Mr. and Mrs. Noah and their sons and their wives and the coupled animals. They no longer muse about what it might be like to live in a big boat with monkeys. Instead, they begin to ask, "Is it true that everyone else and all of the other animals in the entire world died? God did that?"

When children begin to ask these kinds of questions about the story of Noah's ark, they are encountering what one philosopher calls an "epistemological crisis."[5] An epistemological crisis is when we learn or realize something that throws all of the other things we believe in out of whack. In the child's case with Noah's ark, God looks loving when we draw pictures of the eight smiling people who were saved and the smiling animals who were preserved. God looks quite different when we think that everyone else and all other animals were destroyed. The "God of Love" becomes the "Master of Overkill," who has had enough of this defective beta version of creation and is ditching it in order to unveil a new, revised world. In a child's mind, holding the creation story and the Noah story side-by-side pits the loving God of the creation stories against the angry God of the flood story. The God who brought the world into existence out of the murky waters of chaos now looses those same waters with a vengeance!

I'm using the example of children for two reasons. First, children are honest enough to say out loud what they think, even if it is a passing thought and even if it means that they are walking on the thin ice of saying something that doesn't sound like proper church doctrine. That refreshing honesty stems from a kind of naïveté that children have in reading and hearing stories. They haven't "grown up" to the point of filtering their reactions. Second, I am using the example of children because they are natural-born literalists (although they are able to hold contrary ideas together in ways that would drive an adult literalist crazy). It is their literal reading of the Noah story that causes children to experience a crisis when they get older. One day they might be old enough to accept that some things can express truth without being "true" themselves. But, long before that, children are old enough to know that a worldwide flood is nothing to color pictures about.

So far, I've been pretending that it is only children who go through this kind of crisis with the story of Noah's ark. Now it is time to admit that many adults have the same kind of problems with that story. Some repress those problems; some just accept as a matter of course that God has a really, really mean side; and some are so confounded by this problem that

5. MacIntyre, "Epistemological crisis, Dramatic Narrative and the Philosophy of Science"; and MacIntyre, *Whose Justice? Which Rationality?*, 362f.

they think religion is inherently evil. In each reaction, the problem lies not so much with the biblical story itself, but with the problem of reading poetic texts literally.

If we read the story of Noah's ark poetically, it doesn't magically remove the tension between the rescue of some and the destruction of the rest. It is still a story of a salvation within a disaster, both of which are attributed to God. But, by reading the story poetically, we can see the tension differently. The descriptive words that are in the Noah's ark story are not so much literal descriptions of what actually happened, but are deliberate representations of the descriptions found in both of the creation stories from the first two chapters of Genesis. The very same words that are used to describe the wonder-filled stories about life in the creation story are also used to describe the tragedy-filled story about death in the flood story.[6] From the first creation story (Genesis 1), the phrases "every winged bird of every kind," and "the wild animals of the earth of every kind, and the cattle of every kind, and everything that creeps upon the ground of every kind" show up over and over in the flood story. In the second creation story (Genesis 2), life is described a little differently. There is no mention of wild animals and sea monsters. There is only mention of domestic animals and cattle and birds of the air. And while the "breath of life" is common to both stories, the second story specifically says that God "breathed into [Adam's] nostrils the breath of life; and the man became a living being."

In the Noah story (Genesis 6–9) the words of the two creation stories are woven together to describe living and dying creatures. So, when Noah and the others enter into the ark prior to the flood, the narrative describes it this way:

> On the very same day Noah with his sons, Shem and Ham and Japheth, and Noah's wife and the three wives of his sons entered the ark, they and every wild animal of every kind, and all domestic animals of every kind, and every creeping thing that creeps on the earth, and every bird of every kind—every bird, every winged creature. They went into the ark with Noah, two and two of all flesh in which there was the breath of life. And those that entered, male and female of all flesh, went in as God had commanded him; and the LORD shut him in. (Genesis 7:13–16)

6. In the two creation stories, the stories are laid side-by-side. In the Noah story, the terms of the two creation stories are woven together into one story.

The words used to describe the rescued humans and animals in the ark are words right out of the creation stories. The ark, then, becomes something like a little microcosm of creation by reusing this language. Likewise, when the story describes the destruction that goes on outside of the ark, it uses the language of creation again:

> And all flesh died that moved on the earth, birds, domestic animals, wild animals, all swarming creatures that swarm on the earth, and all human beings; everything on dry land in whose nostrils was the breath of life died. He blotted out every living thing that was on the face of the ground, human beings and animals and creeping things and birds of the air; they were blotted out from the earth. (Genesis 7:21–23)

When we look at the story of Noah's ark poetically—that is, looking at the words to see the meaning beyond them—we begin to see the inherent connection between the creation stories and the flood stories, both for those who were saved and those who were lost. For the saved, the ark is like a microcosm of creation; for the lost, there is something like the undoing of creation. Now we can sense that the punishment of the flood story is much more complex than the loving creator suddenly turning into an angry judge having a really bad day. The same God who enjoyed every step of creation in the first creation story—calling each day's work of creation "good"—is the God who now destroys so much of creation. The same God whose own breath animated the lump of clay and made it a living being in the second creation story is the God whose waters destroy the creatures "in whose nostrils was the breath of life." No wonder the story ends up with God saying in God's heart, "I will never again curse the ground because of humankind, for the inclination of the human heart is evil from youth; nor will I ever again destroy every living creature as I have done" (Genesis 8:21b). When we read it poetically, this a story of God's broken heart.

When we read them literally, stories get flattened out. We get reward or punishment, blessing or curse, and God as good or bad, because literal reading is linear in its scope. When we read poetically, we begin to see how the creation stories and the flood stories are not mere opposites, but retellings in one way or another. When the flood story re-presents the language of the creation stories so deliberately, we get a sense that that punishment can be painful for the punisher, and not just for the punished.

Hearing the language of the creation and flood stories poetically, we can still see the carnage of the flood story, but we can also hear God weeping in the background. Poetic language can express the depth of a situation where God judges and God cries, all at the same time.

Reading biblical texts poetically does not erase all of the troubling questions that many of these texts evoke. But, at least reading poetically can steer us away from the wrong questions to real questions that account for mixed feelings and stories that can be both comic and tragic at one time. When the Scriptures speak of God's intentions, particularly when it involves God's judgment, those texts are almost always written poetically. Let's look at one very popular text for Left Behind Theology and see how it might look if we read it poetically, instead of literally. But first, a story.

How to Give a Teenager Nightmares

I was in my early teens and my cousin's church was hosting a movie in their sanctuary about the "rapture" called *A Thief in the Night*. It was a hot summer on the Virginia coast and either someone forgot to arrive at the church early enough to crank up the air conditioner or the air conditioner simply was not up to the task of cooling that sanctuary in that heat. Or, something else was afoot. I only mention the heat in the sanctuary because it gives us a feel for the times. There was a very popular movie in theaters at that time about an earthquake that featured large bass speakers inside of the walls of the theater—called "sense-surround"—that roared during the earthquake and actually made the theater shake a bit. Oohh, exciting, almost like being there. If they had only dropped random chunks of concrete, we would have had the full experience! That was the spirit of the times at the movies: do something to the room to create the full experience.

It seems that instead of using bass speakers to create "sense-surround," my cousin's church was aiming for a similar effect called "hell-around," a heat sensation that almost makes you feel the licking flames themselves. So, it was sitting in the heat of this theatrical innovation that we watched a movie about the perils (in the most literal sense) of being "left behind."

The movie began with a husband shaving while his wife was still in bed. She is awakened and notices the odd noise of the husband's electric razor, buzzing in the bottom of the sink. The wife had been steeped in enough Left Behind Theology to figure out soon enough that the "rapture" has come and she had been left behind. Then, she sees on the television that all kinds of people have suddenly disappeared. Their sudden absence caused great confusion and mass terror. And that is just the beginning.

It was a tolerable movie that certainly met its goal of inducing a series of nightmares in young teenagers who watched it while sitting amongst the flames of hell in an overheated sanctuary. Particularly for those of us who had heard sermon after sermon about the pre-tribulation "rapture," the movie depicted very graphically what we had been taught to expect. Of course the movie was followed by an altar call, which was very well attended. The reason that we were so frightened by this movie—in a way different from how we were merely entertained by other popular catastrophe movies about fires, earthquakes, sharks and the like—is because this movie was "based on the Bible."

"One Will Be Taken, the Other Left": A Visit to Literal Land

The key phrase from the Bible that gives Left Behind Theology its edge is from the twenty-fourth chapter of the Gospel of Matthew. It is here that we encounter the repeated phrase that when the Son of Man comes, "One will be taken and the other left" (verses 40–41). In Left Behind Theology, "One will be taken and the other left" means that two people will be standing there side by side, going about their business, when suddenly one of them will be "swept away" in the "rapture," while the other is still standing there saying, "Now where did she go?" It is this one—the confused one, the one who is not ready—who misses the "rapture" and is "left behind" to face awful tribulations. It is a very neat idea and it evokes an enormous amount of anxiety about readiness: "Be ready or, at any given moment, others will be swept away in the 'rapture' and you will be left behind." That is precisely the scenario that was played out in the movie that I saw at my cousin's church, with the husband taken and his wife left behind. Scary? Yes! Effective? Undoubtedly. True? Hmmm . . .

The premise of the movie and other expressions of Left Behind Theology is that we should understand the phrase "one will be taken and the other will be left" literally. So, okay, let's pay a visit to Literal Land and try reading this text literally for a moment. Even when we read the twenty-fourth chapter of Matthew literally, the whole argument and anxiety behind being "left behind" begins to unravel. To begin, the very distinction between who is "swept away" and who is "left behind" is interesting. In Left Behind Theology, it is the righteous who are taken and the unredeemed who are left.

Matthew seems to say otherwise. In Matthew 24, Jesus likens the coming of the Son of Man to the days of Noah, when people were going about their normal business of not watching, not serving God, and not building arks. Instead, they were eating, drinking, marrying, and so forth, in complete oblivion to the disaster that they faced. Then, the flood came and swept them all away, except for Noah and his crew. Did you catch that? Those who are "swept away" in the story of Noah's ark are people and animals who were "swept away" by the waters and *drowned in the flood*! Hello! They weren't "swept away" into the ark and saved. They were "swept away" into death. So, taking Jesus' appeal to the Noah story literally, it is the wicked who are "swept away" and Noah's family—the righteous, the chosen, the survivors, the watching and ready folk—who are "left behind." "Left behind and loving it!" is what I'm guessing, especially if you consider the alternative.

But, please don't take my word for it. Here is the text from Matthew for you to see for yourself: Jesus says, "For as the days of Noah were, so will be the coming of the Son of Man. For as in those days before the flood they were eating and drinking, marrying and giving in marriage, until the day Noah entered the ark, and they knew nothing until the flood came and swept them all away, so too will be the coming of the Son of Man" (24:36–39). What follow these words immediately are the "left behind" words that give Left Behind Theology its emotional force: "Then two will be in the field; one will be taken and one will be left. Two women will be grinding meal together; one will be taken and one will be left" (verses 40–41).

My point is this: Even if we read Matthew 24 literally, the language of being "left behind," from which Left Behind Theology gets all of its emotional force, is actually flipping upside down what Jesus is saying. Still, many of the faithful folk who read Left Behind Theology have become convinced that they want to be "swept away" and not "left behind" because "it's in the Bible." To them, we can only say, "No, it's not."

The worst problem here, however, is that Matthew is really on his way to saying something startling and fabulous with the way that he presents Jesus' words in his Gospel. In other words, Matthew is heading into that territory where one speaks more poetically than literally. As we will see in chapter 5 of this book, Matthew is taking words that originally appeared in Mark's Gospel and is working them into a specific direction with a surprise ending that is completely contrary to Left Behind Theology.

Conclusion

We began this chapter with a pseudo-text from "Zedediah 3:16" and a fictitious letter/response from "Reverend Endall" about the "rapture." One could argue that I am making stuff up, but, in fact, I would argue that Left Behind Theology dabbles in making up texts more than I. At least when I make up a text from "Zedediah," I am willing to admit that it is "for entertainment purposes only." Left Behind Theology produces books, sermons, and movies about a man suddenly disappearing from his wife as a "Bible truth" that "one is taken and the other left." In fact, it is a theology that is built on a misrepresentation of the Scriptures. It pretends to be a literal reading of texts that it pretends were written literally. However, even if we read the text literally—like the reference to those who were "swept away" in the story of Noah's ark—Left Behind Theology distorts the meaning of the words to fit a predetermined theology. We can do better, especially by appreciating how the biblical writers aspired to express depth when speaking of critical issues like the "coming of the Son of Man." And when they turn to poetic speech in order to express that depth, we do best by reading their words poetically. The following chapters will point toward ways that we can do just that.

2

Artificial Intimidation

This Rapture Brought to You by Anxiety, Inc.

ONE OF THE UNMISTAKABLE features of Left Behind Theology is its effectiveness at producing anxiety. My friend Lawrence was taught, as I was, to expect that any second now the "rapture" would occur, the righteous would suddenly be "swept away," and the rest of humanity would be "left behind" to suffer terrible consequences. So, one day Lawrence was working at Sears, where he was a customer service representative back in the day before telephone menus and automated computer systems sneaked across the border and took away all of those jobs. Lawrence was waiting on a customer from behind one of those chest-high counters, where one could fill out paperwork without bending over in front of everyone. Lawrence was proof-checking a form when, suddenly, the customer just disappeared. Just like that, in a twinkling of an eye, the man vanished as if he had been snatched away by a thief in the night. That doesn't happen every day; not even at Sears.

So, what did my friend Lawrence do? He did exactly what a lifetime amalgam of "rapture" sermons, Left Behind movies, and readings from the annotated Scofield Reference Bible trains us to do: He panicked. Lawrence panicked because, as he immediately inferred, the "rapture" had come and he had been left behind to suffer the terrible consequences of the tribulation. And the significant thing about this sudden panic is this: Lawrence was not afraid that he had been left behind because he was an "unbeliever." By all means he had accepted Jesus Christ as his savior, believed with all of his heart, tried to live as a faithful person, and was a very active member of Christ's church. But, the anxiety-laden nature of Left Behind Theology strives against comfort and assurance. The arguments are something like this: Sure, Lawrence was a good man, but good works don't get you into heaven, much less the "rapture." Besides, there are always more works that one has left undone. Sure, Lawrence was a believer, but perhaps he harbored some secret doubts along the way. Can anyone say that she or he never has any doubts? And sure, Lawrence was faithful in attending church every week, but who wasn't back before Barnes & Noble was open on Sunday mornings?

The point is that none of our customary assurances can stand in the face of the anxiety produced by Left Behind Theology. Even those folks who attend high-pulpit churches—where nobody ever says the word "rapture" and people read prayers of confession together every Sunday—are unsafe. To them, Left Behind Theology says, "If you think asking forgiveness each Sunday for 'things done and left undone in thought, word, and deed' is good enough, then you are leaving out that crucial 'thief in the night' clause. What if Jesus comes on, say, Wednesday, when you are right in the middle of committing all of those sins that you will confess on Sunday? It seems that your best hope is that Christ returns about 11:25 or so on a Sunday morning, just after you have repented and just before you sin again." Once again, the joy of good Christian piety is trumped by the anxiety of Left Behind Theology.

When Lawrence's customer suddenly disappeared and Lawrence himself was left behind to see it, the Apostle Paul's notion that "nothing can separate us from the love of God in Christ Jesus" went out the window. What was Paul thinking when he wrote those words? Something had separated Lawrence from the love of God—even if he didn't know what it was and didn't mean to let it happen—because this guy had clearly gone off in the "rapture" and Lawrence was left behind. So, anxiety set in. Lawrence started breathing rapidly and shallowly as all of the movies and books and sermons that he had seen and heard came crashing into his frontal lobe in a monstrous traffic jam.

Then, right in the midst of this momentary fit of anxiety, Lawrence's customer suddenly reappeared! It was as if the guy had been "raptured," but suddenly his paperwork came through and he was immediately rejected. Or, as if God suddenly thought better of it and rescinded the order for the "rapture" itself until a more opportune moment. Maybe God remembered that there was a prophecy buried in the book of Daniel somewhere that hadn't been fulfilled yet.

In fact, Lawrence discovered the real reason for this "rapture/disrapture" as he spoke to the customer. The man had dropped his receipt and had bent over to pick it up, but had a little trouble getting it up off the floor—hence the momentary disappearance. It was just a very common human action that produced in my friend Lawrence a very uncommon anxious reaction.

Lawrence's story from that day at Sears is the kind of story that almost all Christians who have been steeped in Left Behind Theology experience at some point in their lives. Any sudden or unexplained moment of "disappearance" becomes the pretext for immediate anxiety, because that's how we're told we are supposed to live by Left Behind Theology. I had one of those moments myself when I was fourteen, but to tell the whole story I would need to confess to some things that neither my parents nor my children should ever see in print. That's why I gave you Lawrence's story and, while the name has been changed to protect the embarrassed, it is a true story.

There is no doubt that some Scripture passages have the effect of producing anxiety. For example, Jesus' followers are told to "watch," to "be ready," and to be prepared for the one who comes suddenly and without warning. That's anxiety-producing language, no doubt about it. That's why proponents of Left Behind Theology argue that they are only being faithful witnesses to the Scriptures and, if the "rapture" scenario makes us anxious, then so be it. I think there is some truth to their claim and I do not want to imply that Left Behind Theology voices are just making up scary things or that they are theological sadists. The critical questions, however, have to do with the goal and purpose of Scripture's anxiety-producing language.

Here are some good questions to ask when we read and think about anxiety-producing scriptures. Is language really intended to produce a reaction of fear or anxiety? If so, what is the purpose of that fear or anxiety? Is the purpose of any text to make hearers unsure of whether she is truly a beloved child of God? If so, then what are we to make of those scriptures that speak very differently of God's claim on us, that assure us that no one can snatch us from God's hand and that nothing can separate us from God's love? Are we to live within the bipolarity of being alternately anxious one moment and reassured the next?

I suggest that by keeping these kinds of questions in mind, we encounter a thin line in the Scriptures between seriousness and anxiety. There is a kind of warranted seriousness that is rightly produced by the Scriptures and there is a kind of unwarranted anxiety that is wrongly produced from misreading the Scriptures. Unless we are convinced that God wants us to become neurotic, angst-ridden, paranoid persons—going into a panic because a customer drops his receipt on the floor—we should assume that the kind of response that rightly comes from "watch and be ready" texts has a purpose that is not in conflict with the constant assurances that we hear throughout the Scriptures that "God's steadfast love endures forever." The purpose of this chapter is to provide a way for us to read scary texts within the ongoing assurance of God's steadfast love. To that end, we will look at how the Scriptures themselves use two different voices—one of which is as scary as any of the favored Left Behind Theology texts—in order to describe a single event. But first, let's play a game.

To Tell the Truth

Many years ago, there was a television game show called *To Tell the Truth*, where three people would dramatically step forward into the spotlight and say something like, "My name is Fred Borscht." Fred Borscht, in this instance, would be someone who was known for doing something noteworthy or curious, but whose face the panelists would not know. The panelists' job was to ask questions that the contestants would answer, but only the real Fred Borscht was required to answer them truthfully. In the end, the panel would guess which one of these three persons was the real Fred Borscht and which two were destined to hell for being disgusting lying miscreants. (In the early days of game shows the rewards were smaller, but consequences were much more serious.)

To Tell the Truth reflected a common feeling within our culture that, if there are three different ways of talking about one thing, at least two and maybe even all three of them have to be wrong. So, let's play "To Tell the Truth." The "contestants" in this case all claim to be describing a famous murder! Let's see if we can spot the truth-teller from the liars.

Contestant Number One:

The eyelids and surrounding parts of the face were greatly ecchymosed and the eyes somewhat protuberant from effusion of blood into the orbits. . . . The ball entered through the occipital bone about one inch to the left of the median line and just above the left lateral sinus, which it opened. It then penetrated the dura mater, passed through the left posterior lobe of the cerebrum, entered the left lateral ventricle and lodged in the white matter of the cerebrum just above the anterior portion of the left corpus striatum, where it was found.

Contestant Number Two:

[S]tretched upon a rough framework of boards and covered only with sheets and towels, lay—cold and immovable—what but a few hours before was the soul of a great nation. . . . There [the ball] lay upon the white china, a little black mass no bigger than the end of my finger—dull, motionless and harmless, yet the cause of such mighty changes in the world's history as we may perhaps never realize. . . . [Regarding the brain:] As I looked at the mass of soft gray and white substance that I was carefully washing, it was impossible to realize that it was that mere clay upon whose workings, but the day before, rested the hopes of the nation.

And finally, Contestant Number Three:

O powerful, western, fallen star! O shades of night! O moody, tearful night! O great star disappear'd! O the black murk that hides the star! O cruel hands that hold me powerless! O helpless soul of me! O harsh surrounding cloud, that will not free my soul!

Well, believe it or not, each of these three contestants is claiming to be describing the effects of the same murder. But, while contestant number one speaks of "the anterior portion of the left corpus striatum," contestant number two zeroes in on "the soul of a great nation" and contestant number three describes "the black murk that hides the star!" Can they possibly be talking about the effects of the same single murder? Or, are two of them lying?

In fact, each contestant is talking about the death of President Abraham Lincoln. Contestant number one is Dr. J. J. Woodward, in his formal report of the autopsy of President Lincoln. Contestant number two is another physician who helped perform the autopsy, Dr. Edward Curtis, but his words are not from a formal report. They are from a letter that he wrote to his mother about the autopsy.[1] And, finally, contestant number three is Walt Whitman, in a poem called "When Lilacs Last in the Dooryard Bloom'd,"[2] one of several poems that he wrote after the president's assassination.

So, the assumption that lies at the root of the television show *To Tell the Truth* simply does not apply for our contestants. They are all telling the truth, even though they tell vastly different things. We can say that the account from contestant number one, Dr. Woodward, is more precise and medically detailed as he follows the path of the bullet with excruciating detail into President Lincoln's brain. When I say "excruciating," I mean it is unclear whether we should grab a dictionary or a barf bag when we read it. Still, I think the U.S. would be a better country if every schoolchild had to memorize Dr. Woodward's report. If nothing else, the quality of small talk at most parties would be elevated with a single mention of the word "ecchymosed."

And even though contestant number two, Dr. Curtis, reaches far outside of the bounds of his profession when he speaks about the dead president as "the soul of the nation," his account is also true in a sense. Much more than his colleague's sterile report, Dr. Curtis gives an incredible impression of what it must have been like for those men to perform the autopsy of this president in such a sudden moment of grief.

Finally, contestant number three, the poet Whitman, gives the least literal but what might be truest account yet of President Lincoln's death. Whitman's manner of expressing truth is more comprehensive in scope than Dr. Woodward's precision and even Dr. Curtis's grief. This president's death is, for Walt Whitman, an event that changes everything, from the starry sky above to the deepest soul within. It should be noted that even though no western star was observed to have fallen, and no great star is recorded as having disappeared (or disappear'd, for that matter), no one has ever accused Walt Whitman of lying about these astronomical matters.

Holding these three true accounts of President Lincoln's tragic death side by side, we can see that it is possible to tell a single story truthfully, yet differently. But, it is also obvious that what might be true in one sense would be ridiculously untrue in another. Imagine Dr. Woodward writing in his autopsy report that there was an "effusion of blood in the western,

---

1. Dr. Woodward's report and Dr. Curtis's letter are posted online at http://nmhm .washingtondc.museum/exhibits/lincoln/casualty_of_war4.html.

2. Available online at http://www.bartleby.com/142/192.html.

fallen star." Mixing the clinical voice and the poetic voice would have been a bad prescription for the good doctor's career, I think.

Holding these accounts side by side also helps us to see that the wild cataclysmic language of Mr. Whitman's poetry—which would be scarier than all get-out if it came out of a national weather service forecast—is scary language that is not intended to be scary. When President Lincoln was killed, there were no literal cruel hands that reached up and held Mr. Whitman powerless and no literal "harsh surrounding cloud" that took his soul prisoner. The real intent of Mr. Whitman's poetry is lost and trivialized when we treat it as if it was meant to be taken literally.

Part of what makes people like my friend Lawrence so angst-ridden is the attempt in Left Behind Theology to act like the poetic voice of the Scriptures is practically the clinical voice, to treat a phrase like "O, great star disappear'd" as if it were meant to be taken as literally as the "penetration of the dura mater." In the biblical text, Left Behind Theology treats phrases like "the Son of Man coming in the clouds" as literally as "Jesus wept." But, the folks who told the biblical stories and eventually put them into the written word approached things differently. Like Dr. Woodward and Mr. Whitman, they understood that things can be described truthfully in more than one way. And for the biblical writers, the poetic voice is a true and accurate way of speaking about serious matters. The poetic voice is not true only after it is treated as some kind of coded puzzle that has to be teased apart in order to be understood non-poetically. It is true even if nothing about it is any more actual or "real" than Whitman's "black murk that hides the star."

Let me demonstrate what I mean by exploring a single-event series in the Scriptures that is described in two very different voices. If we can appreciate the "two ways of telling the same thing" demonstrated by this text, we are well on our way to see how many texts of the Scriptures are misunderstood by Left Behind Theology as communicating anxiety, when they should communicate seriousness.

Battle Tales and Truth Telling

The life and exploits of David, the humble shepherd boy who became Israel's greatest king by God's election, makes for some memorable stories. From the unlikely event of young David defeating the battle-tested giant named Goliath, through the hazardous moments when the reigning King Saul sought to take David's life, through the sordid story of lust, rape, deceit, and murder for a woman named Bathsheba, David's stories have been told, read, and remembered in unforgettable ways for years. The typical way that David's stories were written is through narrative, where the narrator would have insight into things that are said behind the closed curtains of the king's chambers as well as instructions that God might whisper into people's ears. But, there is one part of David's story that is told in two very different ways—through narrative, and through a poetic voice that biblical scholars describe as a "theophany."

First Samuel 18 begins a series of episodes about King Saul's attempts to kill David. Saul was jealous of David for two reasons. First, God had elected David to replace Saul as king. The prophet Samuel brought Saul the message and anointed David, just like he had previously anointed Saul. And David's successful exploits on the battlefield were proof positive that God was now with him specially. Second, while David's victories were helpful to Saul's reign in geopolitical terms, they were giving David a reputation among the people that the king envied and resented. Imagine how a warrior king like Saul felt when all the women hanging around the city gate were singing the new number one hit, "Saul has killed his thousands, and David has killed his ten thousands!" So, Saul gets angry and David goes on the lam, trying to escape Saul's murderous jealousy through means that make the narratives wonderful: sneaking around, benefitting from insider information, using the old "put something in the bed while pretending to be sick" trick, acting crazy, running away, and even defecting for a time to the loathsome Philistines. As the narratives tell the stories, David escapes intact through some very daring, but human means.

Likewise, after becoming King, David leads his people through a series of ongoing wars. David is very good at being a warrior and a king—except for the regrettable Bathsheba incident—and the narratives describe his battle plans, his generals, his mistakes as well as his better choices, and so forth. While these stories make constant reference to God being with David, they are focused on the ordinary human intrigue of making war: mule riders chasing other mule riders, old friends betraying one another, grizzled veterans unenthusiastically taking the life of the young whelp who is trying to earn his battle reputation, and so forth. And, of course, there is the usual war story of a young man who tries to steal his father's throne through a coup, only to meet his demise by getting his afro caught in the branches of a tree and hanging there while his enemies take target practice on him.

My point is this: In the narratives of David's exploits—both his escapes from Saul and his battles as the king—the stories are filled with earthy, thoroughly human detail. While there are constant references to God granting the victory, the means of victory are the stuff of war stories. But, there is another way of telling this story, which makes God more than an occasional consultant and a much more active agent in the battles. And we get that way of telling the story in 2 Samuel 22.

Second Samuel 22 is a psalm that is attributed to David "on the day when the Lord delivered him from the hand of all his enemies, and from the hand of Saul" (v. 1). It is repeated, almost word for word, as Psalm 18 in the Psalter. As a psalm, it is a poetic way of accounting for all of the things that are described narratively in the books of 1 and 2 Samuel. But, while the narratives describe all of the human escapades of stealth and battle, David's psalm describes it quite differently. For example, the psalm speaks of how David cried out to the Lord. And here's the reaction:

> Then the earth reeled and rocked;
>> the foundations of the heavens trembled and quaked,
>> because [God] was angry.
> Smoke went up from his nostrils,
>> and devouring fire from his mouth;
>> glowing coals flamed forth from him.
> He bowed the heavens, and came down;
>> thick darkness was under his feet.
> He rode on a cherub, and flew;
>> he was seen upon the wings of the wind.
> He made darkness around him a canopy,
>> thick clouds, a gathering of water.
> Out of the brightness before him coals of fire flamed forth.
> The LORD thundered from heaven;
>> the Most High uttered his voice.
> He sent out arrows, and scattered them—lightning, and routed them.
> Then the channels of the sea were seen,

> the foundations of the world were laid bare
>
> at the rebuke of the LORD,
>
> at the blast of the breath of his nostrils. (2 Samuel 22:8–16)

Wow, those narratives in 1 and 2 Samuel sure left out all of the cool parts, didn't they? Maybe it's just me, but if I were writing about a battle and the earth reeled and rocked, or God's nostrils began emitting smoke, or fire from heaven started frying Philistines all over the battlefield, I think I might have included that in the story at least once! But, none of the narratives so much as mention any of these fine details. In fact, the narratives suggest that if you or I happened to be standing there, watching the battles of David with our own eyes, what we would see are sweating horses, bloody warriors, dying men calling for help, scared men looking for a way out, and an occasional crazy-looking man who has caught the battle fever and seems to be enjoying all of this carnage. We would see no fire coming out of the heavens, no thunder shaking the earth, no smoke or clouds and—darn it all!—not even God riding on a cherub. I would pay to see God riding on a cherub, but the narratives do not record any of the fascinating descriptions that are in David's psalm, just like Dr. Woodward did not record Walt Whitman's fallen western star in Abraham Lincoln's skull.

And yet, like the poet Walt Whitman, the psalm of David is not lying when it describes God's presence in the battlefield. The psalmist is not slipping into a dementia-filled dotage or trying to enhance a legacy or any other form of falsehood. The language of this psalm is that of what biblical scholars call a "theophany," literally, an "appearance of God." The point of the theophany is not to describe what happened "on the ground," so to speak; it is to make the theological claim that God really is invested in Israel's history, regardless of what one sees on the ground. In this instance, the rocking and reeling world, the smoky heavens, and all of the other poetic expressions are ways of saying that David's exploits matter, that the question "Who is king and who is not?" matters, and that the sweaty, bloody brutishness of war means something beyond the sweat, blood, and brutality. Robert Alter says that poetry "is not just a set of techniques for saying impressively what could be said otherwise. Rather, it is a particular way of imagining the world."[3] The poetry of 2 Samuel 22 is a worldview: It

---

3. Alter, *Art of Biblical Poetry*, 151.

is a faith-filled way of describing the same reality that is described differently in the narratives of 1 and 2 Samuel. As a theophany, it is a description of God's immersion in what might otherwise simply be perceived as earthy, earthly stuff.

The Scary Language of the Scriptures

The relationship between the narratives of 1 and 2 Samuel and the poetry of 2 Samuel 22 illustrates precisely the point I want to make about the scary language of the Scriptures. The Scriptures often use frightening poetic language to point beyond "life as we know it and see it" to "life as we can only imagine it." They point to life as God-filled and events as God-driven, even if—on the ground—the view and the experience is much different. The ancient reader of these words understood that David's battles were filled with spear tips and dented shields, not earthquakes and smoky heavens. The reader would have known that neither David nor David's enemies, like Saul or the Philistine armies, would have actually seen God swooping down on the back of a cherub. So, to return to our question about the scary language of the Bible: Why does 2 Samuel 22 use the scary language of fire, smoke, and lightning darts coming from the sky, even when that's not what people on the ground actually see?

Remember that scholars call the language of this psalm a "theophany." The "theo" in that word is from the Greek word for God, just like in the word "theology." And the "phany" is from the Greek word for "appear," as in the word "epiphany." The theophany, then, is a way of making the hidden "God angle" of an event apparent. So, for example, when Saul tries to kill David because David is a threat to his own position as king, most history books would treat Saul's actions as fairly typical of how monarchs often worked back in those days. But, the psalm in 2 Samuel 22 discloses how God regards Saul's actions with the horrifying words, "God was angry." Saul has the nerve to oppose God's election! Saul has the nerve to think that he can murder David when God has explicitly chosen David to be the king of God's own people! Saul—whom God once elected as king himself—thinks he is now in charge instead of God! And for those reasons, the psalm uses "theophanic" language to describe the seriousness of Saul's actions. This is more than a paranoid monarch doing what paranoid monarchs do. This is Saul overstepping his bounds and trying to usurp God's intentions for Israel. That's serious.

When reading poetic language in the Scriptures, it is important to avoid the kind of interpretation that Left Behind Theology often trumpets: breaking the secret code. There is not a one-to-one relationship between the poetic imagery and the "real" events that only the clever insider can figure out. It would destroy the meaning of the psalm to argue that "God's smoking nostrils" = "the heavy breathing of the losing army," or that "God riding on a cherub" = "David's horse being faster than a Philistine's mule." That's not how poetic language works. For this psalm, the cumulative effect of the words offers a picturesque way of seeing how God is at work among God's elect, even when it is not evident from the ground. It is only by eschewing any attempt to make a one-to-one correlation between the poetic images and the literal events that one can appreciate the level of depth and seriousness that the scary language of a theophany adds.

But, we still have not quite answered our question of why the *Scriptures*, "the writings," use scary language. So far, I've been using "words," "speech," and "language" interchangeably, but now I will be more specific. As *written* expressions of what once might have been spoken poetry it is not for David's sake that the Scriptures speak of what God is up to behind the scenes. David is dead by the time these words are written and collected as Scriptures. So is Saul and so are all of those Philistine armies. The scary language of this theophany is not written at all for the sake of the people *in* the story; it is written for the sake of the people *reading* the story. And to pursue our question of why the Scriptures use scary language, we need to turn our attention to the audience for whom the Scriptures were written.

When we turn our attention from the characters of the biblical story to the audience to whom the text was written, we are looking to see what is going on in the world "behind the text." Most biblical scholars argue that, while the psalm in 2 Samuel 22 is attributed to David—let's say around the tenth century BCE—this psalm was probably written at a much later date, during a time of extreme duress in the life of the people of Israel known as the "exile." The exile refers to a time when many Jews were deported from Jerusalem to Babylon in 597 BCE, which was followed by the destruction of Jerusalem in 587 BCE. It was a period when Israel's three most important signs of God's protection and favor were lost: they no longer possessed the Promised Land, the throne that once held King David was emptied of God's elected king, and the temple as a sign of God's presence among them was destroyed. It was during a desperate and disheartening time that the psalm in 2 Samuel 22 was written. As J. Clinton McCann says, "These hyperbolic descriptions obviously exceed the reality that any Israelite or Judean king actually experienced. In short, the descriptions affirm Israel's faith in God's rule amid circumstances that seem to deny it."[4] For the people in exile, whose land was possessed by Babylon, whose rulers were now Babylonian puppets, and whose temple was in ruins, it seemed like Babylon's military strength was proof positive that Israel's God was dead and the Babylonian gods were the true gods of power and might. And the people—quite naturally—longed for a return of Good King David, who loved God and who was a successful king. Maybe a king like David would be able to amass an army and overcome Babylon! But here, at the end of all the narratives of David's exploits, was this startling reminder that what made David such an effective king was not his military savvy; it was God's hidden power behind him. And that is where the forlorn people in exile could put their hope.

I invite you to keep in mind Walt Whitman's image of Abraham Lincoln's death as the "fallen western star" and David's poetic image of the heavenly fireworks display in 2 Samuel 22 as we look at some of the scarier texts of the Scriptures throughout this book. My point is not to say that scary texts are not really scary. Indeed, the language is scary, even mortifying at times. My point is that the scariness of those texts often points toward something that is different from simply being frightening. What makes many of these texts scary is not that they describe what God is going to do exactly the way that we would perceive it "on the ground." If that were the case, then we would have good reason to doubt that God's steadfast love endures forever. We would also have reason to live as anxiously as my friend Lawrence was on the day that the sudden disappearance of his customer led him immediately to imagine that he had missed the "rapture" and was doomed. What the scariness of many scary biblical texts point to is not anxiety, but a way of maintaining hope, even in the most desperate and trying times.

4. McCann, "Psalms," 747.

3

Left Behind Theology and Homotextuality

The Struggle against Textual Perversion

THERE COMES A TIME when people of conviction simply have to stand up for what is right. And—although it seems to violate the spirit of our age and go against the grain of the free-wheeling openness that characterizes our "marketplace of ideas"—to stand for something that is right often calls for us to stand against something that is wrong, no matter how popular it may be. That is why I have decided to put my reputation on the line and to eschew safe and comfortable boundaries by taking on what I believe is a dangerous evil facing people of faith and good will today: Homotextuality.

For too many years now, the homotextual agenda has been making its way into our public discourse—in study Bibles, through television shows, and even from pulpits across America. We have elected politicians who publicly embrace homotextuality as an acceptable way of life and who shamelessly pander to homotextuals themselves. Even parents, who have modeled heterotextuality for their children for years, find themselves too intimidated to speak out when their college-age children return home and forthrightly confess that they have joined campus groups that engage regularly in homotextuality. I'm telling you, homotextuality is ruining the church, it is ruining our culture, and it is stabbing some of the greatest foundations that made us who we are today in the back. And I invite you to join me in resisting homotextuality, no matter how popular and respectable it may seem to be.

Before you decide for yourself, let me clarify what I mean by the term "homotextuality," since the practice of homotextuality has sneaked in through the back door almost undetected. "Homotextuality" is comprised of two parts. The prefix "homo" means "same." Believe it or not, one of the first great controversies of the Christian church was over this prefix.[1] And now, here we are these many years later, once again seeing the church tortured by this selfsame prefix! Of course, the root of the word "homotextuality" is "textuality," which refers not so much to a text itself as to the way one reads a text. So, the most literal meaning of the word "homotextuality" simply means "to read texts as the same." And that is precisely what I see as the problem that is attacking the church today and spilling over into our society itself: The tendency to read the Scriptures as if they all say essentially the same thing.

Let me offer you a harmless example. Every Christmas pageant under the sun has three great movements that converge in the final scene where Joseph and Mary, the shepherds, and the magi are gathered around the baby Jesus singing, "Go, Tell It on the Mountain." Joseph and Mary travel to Bethlehem at the decree of Caesar Augustus in order to register for the census; the shepherds travel over to the stable in Bethlehem from some fields in that same region at the instruction of an angel; and the magi travel from the East because they have seen a new star at its rising and have discerned from that star that a new king of the Jews has been born. It was Herod's consultants who sent the magi to Bethlehem itself, where they see the star once again. The three journeys converge on the stage for a final scene, and it is lovely and there is nothing that I am going to say here that takes away from its loveliness—especially when the characters are portrayed by children.

To get to this final scene, however, we have to be willing to take certain liberties with the Gospel according to Matthew. Most of the setting of the Christmas pageant is based on Luke's Gospel. That's where we get things like the imperial census that forces Joseph and Mary to travel to Bethlehem, the lack of any available rooms in the inn, the swaddled baby

---

1. The controversy was over whether Jesus was the "same substance" (*homo-ousion*) or of "like substance" (*homoi-ousion*) with God. Apparently, one has to answer this question correctly to go to heaven.

in a manger, the "multitude of heavenly host," and the night sky under which the shepherds hear about the birth. And thank goodness that we have such a fine storyteller in Luke, because Matthew really scores an "epic fail" as a Christmas pageant writer. In fact, in Matthew's Gospel, Jesus' birth is told as a passing event: "When Joseph awoke from sleep, he did as the angel of the Lord commanded him; he took [Mary] as his wife, but had no marital relations with her until she had borne a son; and he named him Jesus" (Matthew 1:24–25). "Until she had borne a son"? Are you kidding me? That's Matthew's idea of a Christmas story? It's pretty clear that if Luke had not written his gospel we would not even have a Christmas pageant because it would be too boring.

The one real contribution that Matthew offers to the Christmas pageant is the journey of the magi from the east. Since the magi are directed from Herod's palace to Bethlehem to find the child, the pageant quite nicely folds Matthew's story into Luke's story for the rousing final scene at the manger. However, Matthew ruins the moment, if we let him.

In Matthew's Gospel, when the magi arrive they do not find the babe wrapped in swaddling clothes lying in a manger. Matthew says, "On entering the house [house!], they saw the child with Mary his mother; and they knelt down and paid him homage" (Matthew 2:11). If we were all experienced in reading biblical Greek, we'd notice that Matthew uses the term *paedion* to describe Jesus, which can mean anything from an infant to an older child. Luke, on the other hand, uses the word *brephos*, which refers to an embryo, a fetus, or a newborn. And, in Matthew's story, Herod has all of the Jewish children ages two and under killed, based on the exact time that the star first appeared to the magi while they were still in the East. The implication is that, in Matthew's story, Jesus might have been two years old by the time the magi arrived.

But a two-year-old Jesus sitting in a house with his mother at the arrival of the magi would just ruin the Christmas pageant, wouldn't it? And leaving the magi out of the pageant altogether is simply not an option. Good heavens, what would we do with the really tall and shy kids in Sunday School if we couldn't throw a beard on them and let them walk around looking wise and solemn? Nope, in situations like this, homotextuality is our friend. We can pretend as though Matthew and Luke are essentially telling the same story about the same sweet little baby Jesus, squeeze it all into the same time frame, and blithely overlook any real differences between them in the name of preserving a heartwarming tradition. That's how homotextuality works. It pretends that writers are telling the same story, even if they are not.

In other situations, homotextuality is not our friend. In fact, it is a destructive way of reading the Scriptures to take richly detailed stories and flatten them out in order to make them describe the same thing. And that is one of the primary biblical problems with Left Behind Theology, especially when it comes to the book of Daniel, one of the richest and most curious books of the Hebrew Bible. Consider this comment by Thomas S. McCall, writing in the *Tim LaHaye Prophecy Study Bible*: "The book of Daniel stands as a monument of predictive truth. It is often compared to the book of Revelation and in truth, the book of Revelation cannot be understood apart from the foundations laid in the book of Daniel. An understanding of Daniel and Revelation constitutes the basics of Biblical prophecy."[2]

I certainly agree with Mr. McCall that Daniel stands as a "great monument of truth." The problem of homotextuality arises when Daniel is described as a monument of "predictive" truth. By arguing that Daniel is predictive, the relationship between Daniel and Revelation—as well as many other books of the Bible—becomes a flat, one-directional, one-dimensional flow from a prediction to a fulfillment. The prediction was made in the past; the fulfillment comes at a later time. It makes Daniel appear to be the greatest prophet ever in the Hebrew Bible, because he had visions, dreams, and prophecies that began unfolding during the New Testament era and continue to unfold today.

However, this way of reading Daniel does a disservice to the book of Daniel as well as to the New Testament writers who read and employ Daniel in many different ways. Daniel is a very multifaceted book and to reduce it to simple "prediction" is to lose its richness. This chapter will offer a "heterotextual" way of looking at Daniel that preserves its richness. In future chapters I will show how the New Testament writers who use Daniel as a way of addressing their moment in time are engaging in intertextuality, not homotextuality, so we should read them as such.

---

2. McCall, "Prophecies of Daniel."

Reading Daniel

When one reads the book of Daniel, two things are immediately clear. First, there is a huge difference between the first and second halves of Daniel. Second, Daniel developed a substance abuse problem in between these two halves. Okay, maybe not a substance abuse problem, but if drugs can't account for the radical differences between the two halves, something must! And that question—"If not drugs, then what?"—has bedeviled biblical scholars for many years.

The differences between the first and second halves of Daniel are differences in tone, writing style, and emphasis. Chapters 1–6 contain narrated stories about the heroic faith that Daniel and his friends maintain while living as exiled slaves in Babylon. And Daniel becomes incredibly powerful because he has the ability to interpret dreams. He even has the ability to tell the king what his dream was and then to interpret it. But the primary emphasis of the first six chapters is on how God is faithful and keeps Daniel and his friends safe while they are living in a foreign land. So, in these first six chapters we have the memorable story of Shadrach, Meshach, and Abednego being thrown into the fiery furnace, the curious story of a disembodied hand appearing at a banquet and writing mysterious words on a wall, and the great story of Daniel sitting at ease in a den amongst hungry lions. Many of those stories end with the foreign pagan king declaring that the Jewish God is indeed the God above all gods. However, after chapter 6 things change.

Chapter 7 begins with only a brief narration: "In the first year of King Belshazzar of Babylon, Daniel had a dream and visions of his head as he lay in bed. Then he wrote down the dream." What follows that introduction is in a different voice than the first six chapters: Daniel is no longer referred to in the third-person voice by a narrator, but is mostly the narrator himself. Moreover, Daniel is no longer interpreting other peoples' dreams, but is the dreamer himself. In fact, Daniel is no longer able to interpret dreams, but must rely on others to interpret their meaning.

In addition, Daniel's personality seems to change somewhat. Gone is the stoic man in exile who eats bread and water and maintains his prayer life even while living under the threat of death. In the second half of the book, Daniel is a wine drinker. We know that because he takes a break from drinking wine to fast at one point. Likewise, gone is the faith-filled hero, because Daniel is now a visionary who trembles at the sights of his visions and is in constant need of being encouraged to stay strong. Even the whole nature of the book of Daniel changes with chapter 7. No longer is it a collection of heroic narratives that read like stories that were once told aloud and only later put into print. Instead, the last half of Daniel is self-consciously described as a *book*, something written that is sealed up for no one to see or hear until the right time.

To really get a feel for the differences between chapters 1–6 and chapters 7–12 of Daniel, try this thought experiment: You've been asked to teach a Sunday School class on Daniel to six-year-olds. Since the Sunday School program is badly underfunded, you do not have any curriculum provided for you. All you have is your Bible and an open invitation to go through that scary storage room in the back of the education wing to see if you can find some helpful "teaching aids" that you can use.

"No problem," you think, as you open the book of Daniel, "just look at these great stories!" And in the scary storage room you find some great stuff, from riveting felt board figures of lions in a cave, to some great old songs about those "three Hebrew boys," to a modern Veggie Tales story about Shadrach, Meshach, and Abednego, who are called Rack, Shack, and Bennie! Any time you can spread the Word of God with the help of a talking avocado, you know that you've struck gold. This is going to be fun.

But, then you get to the second half of the book of Daniel and you say to yourself, "What the . . . ?" You comb through the scary storage room looking for at least one teaching aid to tell the vision about a goat whose horn breaks and out of that horn grows four more horns and out of one of those horns grows a little horn that eventually reaches up to the heavens. Believe it or not, there has never been a felt board figure of that goat produced by a Christian publishing company. Ever. Even Veggie Tales left that one alone. The only teaching aid that you can find is an old timeline that jumps from Daniel's time, to Jesus' day, to a bad pope, to Leonid Brezhnev, the old 1970s unibrowed leader of the Soviet Union back when many people thought it was the evil kingdom that God would destroy from heaven. So much for the scary storage room.

Now, as you imagine trying to teach these six-year-olds about the last half of Daniel, you may see two choices. The best-case scenario would be that mild chaos breaks out in the room as they simply quit listening to you and occupy themselves with other things. The worst case would involve their parents forcing you to visit a nearby clinic because the children did listen to you and their parents are convinced that you developed a substance abuse problem in between chapters 6 and 7. The point is, if you are ever asked to teach the book of Daniel to a group of six-year-olds, a wise response would be, "I'll do it, but only the first half."

What this thought experiment forces us to consider is that the differences between the first half and the second half of the book of Daniel are more than just slight changes in the topic. It seems as though the two halves were written by different hands and that there were different issues being addressed. And that is precisely what most biblical scholars believe as well. Here are some quick observations about the literature and history of the book of Daniel that point to how complex and rich it is.

- The oldest manuscripts available for Daniel are written in two different languages. Verses 1:1—2:4a and chapters 8–12 are written in Hebrew, like most of the Old Testament. But 2:4b—7 is written in Aramaic, which was a widely shared written language in the Ancient Near East until the Greeks conquered that part of the world.[3] Note that these Hebrew and Aramaic sections do not coincide perfectly with the division that I have already pointed out between chapters 1–6 and 7–12.

- Some scholars argue that the Hebrew sections of Daniel show signs of having been translated into Hebrew from Aramaic. Those scholars would argue that the entire book was in Aramaic at one time, which would date the book much later than Daniel's life.

- There are several "loan words" in Daniel that are Persian in origin, which also argues for a later date.

- Therefore, many biblical scholars do not believe that the book of Daniel was written during the time when Babylon destroyed Jerusalem and took many Israelites into exile, which is the period that the first six chapters are about.

- Many biblical scholars believe that the book of Daniel was written centuries after the exile, during the reign of a certain Antiochus IV Epiphanes, which is what the last six chapters are about.

3. Smith-Christopher, "Daniel," 19.

All in all, what we have with the book of Daniel is a complex, multilayered text with stories about heroic faith during the exile as well as perplexing visions that offered words of encouragement during a much later time. At least that is the general summation embraced by most biblical scholars using the best means of biblical study. So, the question arises, how does Left Behind Theology end up flattening this multilayered text into a one-dimensional scheme of "predictive truth"?

A Homotextual Reading of Daniel

When Left Behind Theology reads Daniel the primary emphasis falls on four verses, Daniel 9:24–27. The speaker is "the man Gabriel" who came to Daniel "in swift flight" during the evening sacrifice and gave him these words that he might understand his vision:

> Seventy weeks are decreed for your people and your holy city: to finish the transgression, to put an end to sin, and to atone for iniquity, to bring in everlasting righteousness, to seal both vision and prophet, and to anoint a most holy place. Know therefore and understand: from the time that the word went out to restore and rebuild Jerusalem until the time of an anointed prince, there shall be seven weeks; and for sixty-two weeks it shall be built again with streets and moat, but in a troubled time. After the sixty-two weeks, an anointed one shall be cut off and shall have nothing, and the troops of the prince who is to come shall destroy the city and the sanctuary. Its end shall come with a flood, and to the end there shall be war. Desolations are decreed. He shall make a strong covenant with many for one week, and for half of the week he shall make sacrifice and offering cease; and in their place shall be an abomination that desolates, until the decreed end is poured out upon the desolator.

A key phrase from these verses is the phrase "an abomination that desolates." That phrase appears twice more in Daniel, as well as in other books written about the same time that the book of Daniel was written, and later, in the New Testament. We will track that phrase into the New Testament in later chapters. The other distinguishing features of these verses are the numbers: seventy weeks, broken into seven weeks plus sixty-two weeks plus one more week that is divided between a first half and a second half. Since the ending point of these time markers is war and desolation, it is natural for the reader to ask, "When will all of these things take place?" And the thing itself, the central prediction in these verses, is that "the prince who is to come shall destroy the city and the sanctuary." By that, we think of the city of Jerusalem and the temple.

Among the adherents to Left Behind Theology there are various opinions over the exact way to understand these time markers in Daniel's ninth chapter, but there is significant agreement on the general understanding of it within a prediction-fulfillment matrix. For example, Harold Lindsell argues that the phrase "abomination that desolates" has three different fulfillments. In Lindsell's reading, Daniel had this vision and wrote it down during the sixth century BCE, following his captivity and exile under the Babylonian king Nebuchadnezzar. So, the "prediction" takes place in the sixth century BCE and then is fulfilled in three ways. First, it is fulfilled in 168 BCE, when a general, Antiochus IV Epiphanes, profaned the rebuilt temple by slaughtering a pig on the altar as a sacrifice to Zeus. Second, it was fulfilled in 70 CE when the Romans destroyed the temple in Jerusalem. Finally, the third fulfillment still is waiting to take place. As Lindsell says, "The third fulfillment is yet future; it may come during the time of the great tribulation."[4]

So, the first question that we can rightly ask about Lindsell's interpretation of Daniel 9:24–27 is, "Why three 'fulfillments'?" Daniel does not say, "And behold this prediction shall be fulfilled thrice." No, the idea of three fulfillments is certainly an invention. Without reading Harold Lindsell's mind on this interpretation, let me offer these reasons why Left Behind Theology posits three interpretations of Daniel's vision.

First, it is undeniably the case that when Antiochus IV Epiphanes desecrated the temple by entering the holiest place to offer an unclean animal as a sacrifice to a pagan god, this vision was enacted with incredible accuracy.[5] So, it makes sense for Left Behind Theology to consider Antiochus's act to be a fulfillment of this vision.

But, there's a problem. Left Behind Theology cannot just say, "Daniel's prophecy from the sixth century BCE was fulfilled four hundred years later," because the New Testament—written two hundred years after

---

4. Lindsell, *NRSV Harper Study Bible*, 1293.

5. By the way, this incredible accuracy is exactly the reason why many biblical scholars say that the latter part of Daniel was actually written during the time that Antiochus IV Epiphanes was desecrating the temple. I'll say more about that later.

Antiochus desecrated the temple—picks up the language of "the abomination that desolates" and treats it as a future event, not a past event. So, if Daniel is predictive, Left Behind Theology cannot be content letting Antiochus alone be the fulfillment of Daniel's vision. The solution is to posit that Antiochus did fulfill the vision of Daniel 9, but that the vision also had a second fulfillment, after the time of Jesus. Lindsell says that the second fulfillment was when the Romans destroyed the temple in 70 CE, approximately forty years after the death and resurrection of Jesus.

But, those two fulfillments are not quite enough either, because, toward the end of the book of Daniel, Daniel is instructed to "keep the words secret and the book sealed until the time of the end" (Daniel 12:4). The destruction of the temple by the Romans in 70 CE was devastating for many Jews and early Christians, but it was not the end of time. We are, after all, still here living on this earth with the same admixture of joy and sorrow, tragedy and triumph, good and evil that was at hand in biblical times. So, because Left Behind Theology sees Daniel in a prediction-fulfillment scheme, it is compelled to argue that this prediction has not yet been completely fulfilled. The third fulfillment that Lindsell supposes is when the reign of God finally comes and takes place on the earth, which evidently has not happened yet.

My point is that as long as Left Behind Theology insists on reading Daniel in a one-dimensional, homotextual, prediction-fulfillment scheme, Lindsell's arguments make sense. The question is, is that the right way to read Daniel?

A Heterotextual Reading of Daniel

If you walk into any popular bookstore chain and look at the books listed under "Christian inspiration" or "Bible study" or even "Christian fiction," you would get the impression that the prediction-fulfillment scheme is the only way of reading the book of Daniel. That impression is certainly understandable, but it is not true. In addition, you will often see writers who embrace Left Behind Theology accuse scholars who do not read Daniel in a prediction-fulfillment scheme of either not believing in the Bible in general or not believing in "prophecy" in particular. Again, neither of those accusations is true.

I suppose that most of the Left Behind Theology folk would include me under these accusations. But, there are places where I agree with the way that Left Behind Theology folks read Daniel. I agree that Daniel is a very important book, both for its theological content of how God is faithful in times of despair and for its historical value of identifying some of the most traumatic experiences in Israel's faith. I agree that Daniel is a perplexing book, filled with symbolic, radical, and mystical language. I agree that Daniel is "apocalyptic," meaning that Daniel "reveals" what is not seen on the surface. And I believe that Daniel is "prophetic," but more in the sense of truth-telling than fore-telling.

The places where I disagree with the way that Left Behind Theology reads Daniel are many. But, for the sake of clarity, I want to suggest a way of reading Daniel outside of the prediction-fulfillment matrix and allow you to consider whether this way of reading is unfaithful or not. Deeply informed biblical scholars will argue immediately that what I am about to say is largely oversimplified. I plead guilty, but I would point out that all of their highly nuanced, detailed, play-by-play explications of Daniel hurt my head. Sorry. My goal is to keep it simple, without being simplistic or doing violence to the text.

To appreciate the complex layers of the book of Daniel without getting lost in the confusion, let's think in terms of three Daniels, whom we'll call "historic Daniel," "literary Daniel," and "prophetic Daniel." We will begin with "historic Daniel," the young man who was exiled into Babylon and maintained his faith heroically, circa the sixth century BCE. Then, we will look at "literary Daniel," who is the Daniel that appears to us in the stories of the first six chapters of the book of Daniel. You may ask, "Why would you separate the 'historic Daniel' from the 'literary Daniel'?" That is a great question and I will answer that when we get to the literary Daniel below. Finally, we will look at "prophetic Daniel," who is the one to whom I attribute the last six chapters of the book of Daniel and who I think was the "final editor" of the entire book. Remember my remark above that in chapters 7–12 of the book of Daniel the personality of Daniel seems different from in chapters 1–6. I will try to account for that difference when exploring "prophetic Daniel."

Historic Daniel

In 597 BCE something deeply tragic in the life of Judah began to happen. (Judah is the "Southern Kingdom" in greater Israel, where the city of Jerusalem is located as the city of the king and the temple.) Second Kings 24–25 tells the narrative about this grim ordeal, mostly with regard to the kings involved. The Babylonian king Nebuchadnezzar led his army into Judah and utterly defeated them in battle, taking many of the able-bodied and able-minded young people out of Jerusalem to serve Babylon in various ways. Within ten years the Babylonians had thoroughly besieged the city of Jerusalem. Shortly thereafter, they destroyed the temple, burning it along with the king's house and many of the great houses of Jerusalem. As we mentioned in the last chapter, this was a devastating blow for God's people at many levels, not the least of which was the level of faith. If God's favor and election of the Israelites was made known through the gift of the land, the establishment of a king, and the construction of the temple, what did the Babylonian captivity mean for their faith? Many Israelites were asking, as the lament of Psalm 137 asks, "How can we sing the Lord's song in a foreign land?"

Enter "historic Daniel," who, apparently, was part of the exile. I have to say "apparently" because nothing is said about Daniel in the narratives of 2 Kings. Some biblical scholars even wonder if there ever truly was a historic Daniel, but I see no need to question his existence. It seems plausible to me is that there was a man named Daniel, a young Israelite who exhibited heroic faith in the face of the awful circumstances of exile. Stories about Daniel began to circulate that answered the question of how to sing the Lord's song in a foreign land. Those stories continued to circulate for hundreds of years, as the fate of the nation was buffeted to and fro by the geopolitics of the Ancient Near East. In some ways, it seems that the stories of Daniel were cherished stories and part of the faith formation of Israelites, making him a household name for living faithfully under the worst of circumstances. That may be all that we can say about the historic Daniel, and some scholars would argue that I've said more than what is warranted.

Literary Daniel

While the particulars of historic Daniel are vague, we know literary Daniel much better. This is the Daniel whose story is found in Daniel 1–6. The general plot to this story is that literary Daniel is enslaved in the imperial king's house, interprets dreams better than the imperial sages, and eventually is elevated to one of the highest positions in the land.

Wait! Did I just say that the plot of this story is "enslaved in the imperial king's house, interprets dreams better than the imperial sages, and eventually is elevated to one of the highest positions in the land"? People who are familiar with the Hebrew Bible stories will be thinking, "I've heard that plot before!" Indeed you have, in Genesis 39–50. Only, in that story the hero's name was Joseph and not Daniel.

It is certainly apparent that the story of literary Daniel follows the plotline of the story of Joseph quite closely. Or, to look behind the text for a moment, we can say that whoever wrote the story of literary Daniel seems to be following the pattern of the story of Joseph quite closely and deliberately.[6] That is why it is important to keep historic Daniel and literary Daniel distinct from one another. Whoever historic Daniel was and whatever he did may lie beyond our grasp, because the story of literary Daniel in chapters 1–6 of the book of Daniel is clearly a literary act of retelling of the story of Joseph.

However, the narrative of literary Daniel is not an exact retelling of the story of Joseph. Joseph's rise to power in Egypt was impressive, but while he was able to use that power to rescue his family by bringing them to Egypt in the time of a famine, things did not ultimately go well for later generations of this family in the land of Egypt. The story of Moses leading the people of Israel out of Egypt is set up by the fact that, generations before, Joseph had brought them to Egypt. Don't get me wrong: It was a good thing that Joseph survived his ordeal of being sold into slavery and was elevated to a high position from which he was able to rescue his family from starvation during the famine. But it was not so good for his family many years later, as they became enslaved, despised, and oppressed by the Egyptians. So, all in all, Joseph's legacy was ambiguous.

---

6. See Ridge, "Jewish Identity under Foreign Rule," for a close comparison of how Genesis portrays Joseph and how the book of Daniel portrays Daniel.

The ambiguity of Joseph's legacy could be why the narrator of literary Daniel establishes some important differences between Daniel and Joseph. Joseph takes an Egyptian wife and seems by all appearances to be Egyptian. Literary Daniel is more insistent on being distinctively Israelite. He maintains his Israelite habits regarding food, drink, and prayer while in service to various Babylonian kings, and it does not appear that he ever married, leading some biblical scholars to suggest that he was a eunuch.

Likewise, in the story of Joseph, while Pharaoh expresses polite deference to Joseph's family and faith, Joseph's dream interpretation ultimately works for Pharaoh's advantage, making him incredibly wealthy and powerful during a famine. In some ways, Joseph is a tool by which Egypt becomes the empire from which Israel must be rescued years later. On the other hand, Daniel's dream interpretations and other forms of service do not enrich the kings that he serves as much as it impresses them. In the story of Daniel and the Lion's den, the Babylonian king, Darius, had been fooled into sentencing Daniel to death. The story ends up being about whether God would rescue Daniel from the king's stupidity, and even King Darius is pulling for Daniel! Just before Daniel enters the lion's den, King Darius says, "May your God, whom you faithfully serve, deliver you!" The story concludes with Darius making a decree that everyone in his kingdom should tremble and fear before the God of Daniel (Daniel 6:25–27).

Whoever is retelling the plotline of Joseph in the narrative about literary Daniel has no intention of depicting Daniel as conforming to Babylonian ways or being a tool for enriching the Babylonian Empire. For that reason, the similarities and the differences between the Joseph and Daniel stories are important. The stories of literary Daniel answer the question of how to sing the Lord's song in a foreign land. Even in an awful situation like the exile to Babylon, the way of faithfulness is to maintain distinctive Israelite habits and trust that God will deliver the faithful from ridicule, rejection, and even death.

Prophetic Daniel

I am using "prophetic Daniel" to refer to the person who writes the visions, dreams, and script of chapters 7–12 of the book of Daniel. The identity of prophetic Daniel is really the place where the gauntlet is thrown down between Left Behind Theology and other approaches to reading the Scriptures. The proponents of Left Behind Theology insist that the entire book of Daniel was written by the historic Daniel, who was exiled into Babylon in the sixth century BCE.

To be sure, within the text itself, these visions, interpretations, and writings are attributed to historic Daniel's ears, eyes, and pen. But, for reasons literary and historic, most critically thinking biblical scholars today do not attribute the last six chapters of the book of Daniel to the sixth-century BCE figure. I invite you to consider viewing prophetic Daniel not as a sixth-century BCE prophet who saw things that began being fulfilled four hundred years later in the second century BCE, but as a writer from the second century BCE itself. As such, prophetic Daniel is reflecting on the question of how to sing the Lord's song under the awful circumstances of his day. That is, prophetic Daniel is asking, in his time, the very same questions that historic Daniel faced and that literary Daniel's stories address in an earlier context.

After the exile of historic Daniel's day, people were encouraged to trust that God would bring them back to their land. And what a joy it was when the Persian king Cyrus defeated Babylon and allowed the people of Israel to return to their land with all of the treasures that King Nebuchadnezzar had taken when he destroyed the temple. Isaiah goes so far as to refer to Cyrus as God's "anointed one," who saves God's people (Isaiah 45:1).

And yet, in the second century BCE, the people of Israel—once again—have been overrun by a foreign nation. The temple—once again—has been desecrated. And the people's trust in God—once again—has been put to the test. This crisis of the second century BCE is the situation that prophetic Daniel addresses when writing chapters 7–12 of the book of Daniel.

So, we may ask, why would an author do this under the name of Daniel, rather than just in his own name? It is a great question, which I am not able to answer entirely. It was not unusual for people to write under famous pseudonyms in the ancient world, but not primarily as a way of being deceptive or plagiarizing. It seemed to be a way of honoring another and of interpreting what they meant or would have meant if they were still present. So, I propose that we read prophetic Daniel as a person who is trying to offer how the heroic, wise, and faithful Daniel would have answered the question, "How do we sing the Lord's song in this present crisis?"

There were many persons in the second century BCE trying to answer this question. Some said that the people of Israel should fight back as the way of faithfulness. Others felt that such actions would be suicidal and futile. Some wanted the people to quit struggling against the empires around them and to take advantage of what they had to offer, while keeping the essential parts of their faith intact. Others felt that such conformity was a way of forsaking their covenantal relationship with God.

It was among this current of competing arguments that prophetic Daniel wrote chapters 7–12 of the book of Daniel. These chapters use visions to describe how the current crisis came about and interpretations to offer messages of hope regarding how the people of Israel might be saved in the midst of that crisis. Now we will look at some of prophetic Daniel's writings about how people of his day could sing the Lord's song faithfully under the domination of a foreign empire. In particular, we will see how prophetic Daniel introduces two concepts that are powerful for his day and which are adopted by future writers to speak to the disasters of their day.

The "Abomination of Desolation" in Daniel

The phrase "abomination of desolation" comes from the King James Version's translation of Mark 13:14: "But when ye shall see the abomination of desolation, spoken of by Daniel the prophet, standing where it ought not, (let him that readeth understand,) then let them that be in Judaea flee to the mountains." The phrase could be translated in various ways, such as the "desolating sacrilege" or "abomination that desolates" or "abomination that makes desolate," but I am using the words "abomination of desolation" because that is the form that I have seen most often in Left Behind Theology literature. No matter how we translate it, "abomination of desolation" is not a phrase that is used lightly in the Scriptures. And, as the words from Mark's Gospel indicate, the phrase receives its initial meaning in Daniel before it is taken up again in the New Testament.

You may remember from earlier in this chapter that Daniel 9:24–27 plays a key role in Left Behind Theology. In fact, Daniel 9:27 is where we see the phrase "abomination of desolation" for the first time in the

Scriptures. It is part of the message that the angel Gabriel gave to Daniel about the seventy weeks, toward the end of which "the troops of a prince who is to come shall destroy the city [Jerusalem] and the sanctuary." In verses 26b–27 the word "desolation" appears repeatedly to describe the effects of this destructive prince: "Desolations are decreed. He shall make a strong covenant with many for one week, and for half of the week he shall make sacrifice and offering cease; and in their place shall be an abomination that desolates, until the decreed end is poured out upon the desolator."

Looking at Daniel within a prediction-fulfillment matrix, Left Behind Theology argues that the historic Daniel of the sixth century BCE predicted this "abomination of desolation" would take place and that Daniel's prediction has already been fulfilled twice, in the second century BCE and in 70 CE, with one more final fulfillment waiting to happen during the tribulation. While this prediction-fulfillment matrix is quite popular, it is not the only way to read the book of Daniel, and it is not the way that many critically thinking biblical scholars read it.

There is a place, however, where biblical scholars of all stripes agree. And that is that there truly was an "abomination of desolation" that took place in the second century BCE and another one that took place in 70 CE. The question is whether Daniel predicted these events or whether something else is going on. I am going to suggest that something else is going on.

If you recall my distinction between the three Daniels, it is prophetic Daniel who speaks of this "abomination of desolation." And, if you follow my argument, prophetic Daniel was living in the second century BCE, at the time that the event he calls the "abomination of desolation" took place. And what did prophetic Daniel see that he named the "abomination of desolation"? He saw Antiochus IV Epiphanes sell the position of high priest in Jerusalem to the highest bidder. He saw the people of Jerusalem fight back, during a time when Antiochus IV Epiphanes was busy in battle against Egypt. He saw Antiochus IV Epiphanes return and squash the rebellion by making it illegal for Jews to circumcise their baby boys or offer sacrifices. He saw the armies of Antiochus IV Epiphanes raid the temple and take away its sacred treasures. He saw women who had had their babies circumcised killed, with their babies hung around their necks as a sign of what happens when you defy the empire. And, he saw Antiochus

IV Epiphanes go into the holy of holies, erect an altar there to Zeus, and sacrifice a pig on that altar. Daniel's phrase "abomination of desolation" is a pun in Hebrew, a play on the title "Lord of Heaven," given to Zeus on that altar.

When we see this phrase "abomination of desolation" in Daniel 9:27 it is a loaded phrase, filled with absolute contempt and declaring that what Antiochus IV Epiphanes did in the name of the empire was a hideous act against the one true God.

The Son of Man Coming in the Clouds

While Antiochus IV Epiphanes is acting blasphemous and seems to be getting away with it, prophetic Daniel posits an answer to his blasphemy. Desmond Ford, in a very detailed look at the phrase "abomination of des-olation," says that "The 'Son of Man' is heaven's reply to the 'abomination of desolation.'"[7] Ford goes on to describe the opposition between the "*persecuting* abomination" and the "*vindicating* Son of Man." He points out that the Son of Man is "vindicating" and not "vindictive."[8] That is a very important distinction! Ford argues that Daniel, and later Mark, talk about the Son of Man as a vindicator of the persecuted righteous. Left Behind Theology, on the other hand, often portrays the Son of Man as a vindictive destroyer. For prophetic Daniel, the term "Son of Man" is very deliberately an alternative to Antiochus IV Epiphanes and his hideous "abomination of desolation." If you want to see what a vindictive destroyer looks like, argues Daniel, then Antiochus IV Epiphanes is your man.

The Son of Man, on the other hand, looks like this: "As I watched in the night visions, I saw one like a son of man coming with the clouds of heaven. And he came to the Ancient of Days and was presented before him. To him was given dominion and glory and kingship, that all peoples, nations, and languages should serve him. His dominion is an everlasting

---

7. Ford, *Abomination of Desolation in Biblical Eschatology*, 79. Ford uses the Greek words for both "Son of Man" and "Abomination" in this sentence and throughout his work.

8. Ford says that a "vindictive" view of the Son of Man is found in 1 Enoch and 2 Esdras. See, ibid., 80.

dominion that shall not pass away, and his kingship is one that shall never be destroyed" (Daniel 7:13–14).[9]

Notice carefully how Daniel describes this Son of Man: "one like a son of man coming with the clouds of heaven." If we study this description carefully, we should attend to the words "like," "a," and "coming with the clouds" as well as to the phrase "son of man" itself. First, if this is one "like" a son of man, then it would seem that the term "son of man" already has some meaning for Daniel's readers and that this particular figure is being likened to that previous familiarity. Second, it is important to notice the use of the indefinite article—"a" son of man—as opposed to the definite article—"the" son of man. The use of the indefinite article suggests that there are other "sons of man" out there, not just this one. And finally, while the Son of Man comes "with the clouds," it is not the case that he comes from heaven to the battlefield, as often depicted. In this story, he comes with the clouds to the one who is seated on the throne, wherever that is. The only location that we have from Daniel is that the one seated on the throne is in a vision.

So, however the phrase "son of man coming with the clouds" is used in the New Testament, it is important to remember how Daniel uses it originally. This figure is "like" a son of man, he is like "a" son of man, and he comes "with the clouds," but doesn't ever really leave the vision itself. There is no historical moment in Daniel when the Son of Man came from the clouds to receive his kingdom on earth in the same way that the "'abomination of desolation" named Antiochus IV Epiphanes really did desecrate the temple with an abomination. This "one like a son of man" is, as Ford points out, heaven's answer to the "abomination of desolation," but he is not historically present in the same way that Antiochus IV Epiphanes was. And that is crucial. The phrase originally refers to a vision of hope in desperate times, not a battling warrior that really does attack from the sky.

But, while the Son of Man coming with the clouds is a figure that is confined to Daniel's vision, he is a "real" figure in the sense that his kingdom is a legitimate kingdom. In contrast to Antiochus IV Epiphanes, who is depicted in Daniel as uttering blasphemy and bringing destruction in

9. I have opted for the translation of the Aramaic terms for "a son of man" and "the Ancient of Days" in this text, because those are the terms that will be most familiar to people who read Left Behind Theology. The NRSV uses the Hebrew text to translate "a son of man" as "a human being" and "the Ancient of Days" as "the Ancient One."

addition to the "abomination of desolation," the Son of Man is presented before God as a legitimate recipient of dominion, glory, and kingship. He does not win it on the battlefield, through deceit, or by corruption. The Son of Man is granted his eternal reign by God, which is the only way to be crowned legitimately. So, while the Son of Man is confined to Daniel's vision and is not what one might see "on the ground," the vision says something vastly important for Daniel's community. It is a vision about legitimacy—what is right instead of what is wrong, and what ought to be instead of what is actually happening.

The basic message of Daniel 7–12, the "apocalyptic" portion of the book, is that God continues to be in control of history, despite all appearances. And while Antiochus IV Epiphanes appears to be shaking his fist in God's face and getting away with it—causing some to wonder if God exists any more or cares any more—Daniel assures them that Antiochus IV Epiphanes's days are numbered. The real and legitimate king is this "one like a son of man coming with the clouds of heaven."

As I said earlier, it is my opinion that prophetic Daniel actually lived in the second century BCE and witnessed the terrible events of the destruction of Jerusalem and the desecration of the temple. What Daniel saw was the "abomination of desolation" as the temple was desecrated and the holy city was destroyed. What he did not see—on the ground, in reality, and in the way that we customarily speak of "history"—is "one like a son of man coming with the clouds." That is something that is only mentioned as a vision, an assurance of God's providential care, and not as an actual event in real time. Still, as an assurance, this Son of Man is "real" in the sense that God is working God's purposes out, despite all appearances. That is the meaning that this "son of man coming with the clouds" carries from Daniel to the New Testament.

What Would Daniel Do?

All of the events that prophetic Daniel is addressing took place in the second century BCE. It truly was an awful period for the people of Israel. In fact, it would be hard to recall an event that would have challenged their faith and threatened their security so much since the . . . since the . . . since the defeat and exile that Israel suffered back in the sixth century BCE! And if you are a truth-telling prophet, trying to encourage your people during this crisis, what better way than to bring to mind the man named Daniel, who, during that previous exile, demonstrated how to be faithful in awful circumstances. I'm not suggesting that prophetic Daniel lied and tried to convince naïve people that historic Daniel really said all of the things in chapters 7–12 a long time before. I suspect that this was more like an ancient way of handing out "WWDD?" bracelets, encouraging the despondent people to ask, "What would Daniel do?"

It would be hard to overstate how devastating the abominations of Antiochus IV Epiphanes were to the faith of the people of Israel. For a people whose faith had been grounded in how God had provided for them a land, a king, and a temple, the invasion of their land, the imposition of a puppet government, and the desecration of the temple seemed to indicate that the God they knew was no more. It was a time of despair very much like the sixth century BCE, so the turn to Daniel's heroics was very timely. But, it was no "slam dunk" to say, "This is how we should be faithful in these troubling times." There were other options at hand.

Like many persons who have found themselves living under the thumb of a repressive regime, there seemed to be three options for the people of Israel. The first was to follow the old adage, "If you can't beat them, join them!" That is, in fact, what some of the people of Israel had already begun to do. The book of 1 Maccabees says that "many Israelites were in favor of [Antiochus IV Epiphanes's] religion; they sacrificed to his idols and profaned the Sabbath" (1 Maccabees 1:43). Indeed, it would be an enticing option, especially if you buy into the idea that the god with the most powerful army is the most powerful god. Undoubtedly there were some realists among the Israelites who calculated that if you can judge a god by his battlefield exploits, then Zeus seemed to have the clear upper hand on Yahweh. Their response seemed to be "this is 'the new normal,' so go with it!" We could call this the "accommodation" option for how to live under a repressive empire.

This second option for the people of Israel under Antiochus IV Epiphanes was the "fight fire with fire" option, where the only way to defeat tyranny and violence is with a greater force of violence. This is the option that was followed by the Maccabean family, who led a rather successful revolt against the armies that Antiochus IV Epiphanes had left in the garrison at Jerusalem. From age to age, "fighting fire with fire" has been an enticing option for people who live under repression and fear.

Nothing feels more heroic, even heroically faithful, than to fight back on behalf of God. If the cause is right, the argument goes, then the violence is just. That is how we come to love our gunslingers and loathe the others, even though each of them may perform almost identical actions. And, of course, since the refusal to fight back could be as easily grounded in cowardice as it might be in other motives, it is always very difficult for someone to refuse this option, especially if there are zealots at hand ready to risk their own lives for the cause.

Fighting back is not the calculative option that accommodating is. Certainly there is some hope that fighting back will be effective and not suicidal. But, there is always a risk that things will not go well, so fighting back always seems heroic. And, if one were convinced that one is fighting for God, then the possibility that God would make the battlefield a place of working wonders makes fighting back heroically faithful. Certainly the Hebrew Bible is full of stories that imply that God works out God's purposes precisely in this fashion—by raising up militant leaders who are the proverbial Davids slaying Goliaths. Yet, even though this heroic option is the option that the Maccabean family pursued, it is not the option that prophetic Daniel takes.

The third option, which prophetic Daniel argues for, is the way of faithfulness. It might be described best as "trusting in the Lord." I know, I know, this sounds like the "weenie" option. But, before we glare at this option as a weak and ineffectual one, we should make sure that we understand it. To "trust in the Lord" is not to be passive. It may involve confronting God with the brash question, "How long, O Lord?" (Daniel 8:13). It may involve turning to God with repentance and asking forgiveness (Daniel 9:3–19). And it may involve risks because "trusting in the Lord" often means facing the empire and doing things that lead to suffering and death (Daniel 11:33).

To "trust in the Lord" means to live faithfully, to maintain one's practices of piety and worship, to live as if justice matters more than politics, and to act out one's convictions. It is a hard and thankless call, especially when, by all appearances, Antiochus IV Epiphanes and his god Zeus have the upper hand. In other words, trusting in the Lord requires trusting in something that is contrary to appearances. It requires trusting in a vision of how things really are that is different from what one sees with one's own eyes. That is how you sing the Lord's song in a time of catastrophe, according to prophetic Daniel. Incidentally, this idea that God is somehow behind the scenes working all things out providentially was also the point of the Joseph saga in the book of Genesis. The point is expressed most pointedly when Joseph confronts his brothers, who had sold him into slavery years before, and says, "Even though you intended to do harm to me, God intended it for good, in order to preserve a numerous people, as he is doing today" (Genesis 50:20).

So, prophetic Daniel invites his people to frame their questions in terms of "What would Daniel do?" Prophetic Daniel fashions an answer to the question of how to live faithfully and to sing God's praises under a foreign regime by using the voice of historic Daniel as a way of proclaiming God's faithfulness, even in the face of the latest disaster. His bold proclamation is that even someone as seemingly anti-God as this Antiochus IV Epiphanes destroyer is still a part of God's providential care for Israel. In Daniel 9:27, prophetic Daniel says that the "abomination of desolation" will last "until the decreed end is poured out upon the desolator." In other words, prophetic Daniel says that as catastrophic as Antiochus IV Epiphanes's actions are, they are not the last word. God is still in control of history. So prophetic Daniel encouraged the people to "trust in the Lord," even if it means suffering or death.

Don't ask me why, but most of the people that I know don't get energized by the invitation, "Hey, let's live in a way that may get us killed!" Okay, I do know some teenage boys who seem to respond enthusiastically to invitations of that sort, but they usually back out when push comes to shove. And, unless human nature has changed dramatically over the years, it is likely that prophetic Daniel's people needed something a little more persuasive than a death wish if they were going to "trust in the Lord" and resist the empire. That added persuasion is what the visions in Daniel 7–12 provides. Again and again, Daniel's visions portray the present crisis—and the present nemesis Antiochus IV Epiphanes—as moments in a history over which God is fully in control.

Conclusion

What I have tried to describe here is not an exhaustive commentary on Daniel, but a way of looking at Daniel that does not follow the homo-textual prediction-fulfillment matrix so popular in Left Behind Theology.

Instead, I have offered what I would call a "heterotextual" reading, which recognizes some distinction between the historic Daniel of the sixth century BCE, the literary Daniel of the Joseph-like stories of Daniel chapters 1–6, and the prophetic Daniel, the second-century BCE author of Daniel chapters 7–12. My argument is that prophetic Daniel is a voice that is speaking "prophetically" (that is, truthfully) to the despair of his day, not predicting the future. But, of course, prophetic Daniel's words reappear in the Scriptures, namely in Matthew, Mark, and Luke, as well as in the book of Revelation. Particularly, the phrases "abomination of desolation" and "Son of Man coming with clouds" take on new meaning in the New Testament. We will turn to how the New Testament writers employ Daniel's language and imagery in the next chapter, when we introduce yet another alternative to Left Behind Theology's homotextuality, called "intertextuality."

4

Pulpit Fiction

Living through the Great Fibulation

I HAPPENED TO READ a sermon online recently that took me utterly by surprise. It is a sermon based on the apocalyptic images of the Bible, particularly the "abomination of desolation" that we read about in Daniel and Mark. The sermon began with the usual literalist manner of reading the Scriptures—text on top of text, with little regard for who wrote them, when they were written, and what they were addressing; a smattering of history—without much concern for accuracy—to show how the "predictions" have been fulfilled; blaming Israel's historic woes on the Jews' rejection of Christ, but keeping them as the center of God's future attention; and so forth.

The preacher then described how God had partially fulfilled Daniel's and Mark's prophecies by sending the abomination of desolation (via the Roman general Titus) to destroy Jerusalem in the year 70 CE. Finally, the preacher described how the dire words of Daniel and Mark are now being fulfilled in our present day, in a rain of judgment that is even worse than in first-century Jerusalem because it is so deserved by our current generation. Here is his claim:

> Horrible as that act of divine judgment was, it was nothing compared to the abomination of desolation which the Lord God has sent upon this reprobate age in which we live. The things which

happened in Jerusalem 1900 years ago only foreshadowed the judgment of God which has fallen upon this generation. Read the first chapter of Romans, and you will discover that ours is not a generation ripe for the judgment of God. *This generation is under the judgment of God.* I can think of no age, no generation, no circumstance under which the warning of [Mark 13:17] is more appropriate than it is in this day of . . .[1]

I'm sorry to leave you on the edge of your seat, but what would you guess will be the end of the last sentence? What horrific circumstance in present-day existence makes our age, our generation "more appropriate" than ever before to experience the fullness of God's judgment? Remember, if our generation's iniquity is worse than all of the iniquities of past generations, it must be worse than the Inquisition, the conquest of Native Americans, the enslavement of Africans, the Shoah under the Nazi regime, the killing fields of Cambodia, the "disappeared" in Latin America, and even that short-lived reality television show that starred Hulk Hogan. So, how do you think this preacher finished the last sentence above? Brace yourself; you may want to go wash your eyes after you read this. Here is that last sentence in toto: "I can think of no age, no generation, no circumstance under which the warning of verse seventeen is more appropriate than it is in this day of *apostate, freewill, works religion.*" [My emphasis. And well-deserved emphases at that!]

I think I'm going to dress up as an "apostate, freewill, works religion" for Halloween next year, since it is, apparently, the scariest evil imaginable. Of course, while I may score lots of candy from my fundamentalist, hyper-Calvinist neighbors if I showed up in such a costume, I'm guessing that nobody else would even know what I am supposed to be. Would you? Well, in case the phrase "apostate, freewill, works religion" does not disgust you sufficiently, allow me to clarify. What this sermon describes as an "abomination" is the battle cry of an old theological dispute over whether human choice or God's election is primarily what brings salvation. To oversimplify, Calvinists argue that God's election is the key; Arminians argue that human free will is the key. And, of course, those titles are only general directions of a large spectrum of beliefs about the interplay between God's election and human response. The truth is, I'm a Calvinist myself, and I do think most people invest unwarranted confi-

1. Fortner, "Abomination of Desolation."

dence in our ability to make choices. But, it even seems strange to me that anyone would see Arminian theology as the present-day expression of the "abomination of desolation." And yet, with lots of Scriptures and historical references woven together, this sermon finds "apostate, freewill, works religion" to be the very abomination that God has sent as a judgment on our generation.

What is it about apocalyptic imagery that allows it to be applied to darned near anything someone finds objectionable? For years pulpits have been fountains of constant sermons, theories, and claims that the events happening right now among us are exactly what the Scriptures describe as the final signs of the end of the world. Sometimes, the effects have been benign enough, with well-intentioned listeners hearing sermons that have aroused their expectations about the future and left them with a greater fervor for living out their faith in the world. At other times, the effects have been more problematic.

Consider, for example, the case of a certain Mr. Shortridge, who had followed the teachings of Rev. William Miller in the mid-nineteenth century. After studying the prophecies of the Bible over many years, Rev. Miller had concluded that Jesus would return and take his bride (the church) away no later than March of 1843. Thousands of "Millerites" were convinced of the same, and were prepared, some wearing white robes and some even sitting upon their rooftops when the designated day arrived. After midnight, when Jesus had not come back, Millerites recalculated their findings and pushed the date back to October of 1844, when—once again—these disciples of "Millerism" were disappointed.[2] That was the movement and state of mind that the *New York Herald* was addressing when it published this story, titled "Millerism and Insanity" regarding the unfortunate Mr. Shortridge: "We lately published a statement that a Mr. Shortridge, of New Hampshire, had run mad with Millerism, and attempted to ascend to Heaven from an apple-tree, but found the attraction of gravitation too strong for his celestial aspirations, and came to the ground with such momentum as to cause his death."[3]

2. There are many books out about William Miller, ranging from very sympathetic accounts to scathing critiques. The details change depending on whether one is reading the sympathetic or the scathing. My primary purpose in discussing Millerism is to explain the circumstances surrounding the article regarding Mr. Shortridge.

3. This account may or may not be true. The *New York Herald* noted that some witnesses attest to seeing Mr. Shortridge alive after his death was reported, leading

Poor Mr. Shortridge. As someone who shares Mr. Shortridge's irresistible attraction to gravitation, I have to wonder about his willingness to climb a tree in order to facilitate his participation in the second coming of Christ. What is it about apocalyptic texts that seems to allow anyone—serious student of the Bible and nutcase disciple alike—to make detailed, decisive arguments about what the "real" meaning of these texts are, and yet to be so wrong?

The Nature of Apocalyptic Texts

One of the qualities that gives apocalyptic texts their power, and generates such powerful confusion, is that they are highly symbolic. As such, the relationship between the "signs"—comprised of symbolic words and images—and "referents"—that to which the symbols point, is somewhat different than it would be in literal texts. Generally speaking, in literal texts like textbooks, newspapers, or the coroner's report that we read in chapter 2, words are the signs and the common definition of such words are the referents. That is why writers struggle so hard to find "just the right word."

In symbolic texts, the connection between the sign and the referent is less direct and the referent is not necessarily the common definition of the word. When David describes smoke emitting from God's nostrils in Psalm 18, we know what smoke is and we know what nostrils are and we can imagine smoke emitting from nostrils, like in a dragon story. But, it seems to miss the intention of the psalm for us to imagine that David is saying that God really does have a nose and that God's nose really was emitting smoke while David was fighting wars and being rescued from his enemies. Symbolic or poetic language becomes silly when we treat the relationship between the sign and the referent as directly as in literal language.

And yet, even though the connection between signs and their referents is indirect in symbolic language, there *is* a connection. And usually, even with that indirect connection, what symbolic language intends to convey is not too difficult to imagine. It is not difficult to see the smoky nostrils of God as a reference to something like God's anger, which enabled David to be successful on the battlefield. So, while symbolic language does

the *Herald* to say that some of their accounts of the insanity that they associated with Millerism might be mistaken. See "Millerism and Insanty."

not have the direct one-to-one relationship between signs and referents that one might get in a coroner's report or a battlefield news account, there are relationships between signs and their referents and those relationships are where the symbolic language takes on meaning. In fact, as we saw in comparing the coroner's report of Abraham Lincoln's death and Walt Whitman's poetic response to that death, sometimes the indirect, non-literal connection between sign and referent in symbolic language is what gives it such compelling power.

In the symbolic language of Daniel 9, for example, one can read the phrase "abomination of desolation" and see how it is a reference to Antiochus IV Epiphanes and his horrible act of desecrating the temple in 168 BCE. (Other literature of the second century BCE described Antiochus IV Epiphanes's actions with those words also.) Likewise, we will see below that when Mark uses that same phrase in his thirteenth chapter, one can easily say that Mark is using Daniel's loaded symbolic language to refer to the destruction of the temple in 70 CE.

However, the symbolic language of *apocalyptic* texts is different in one way from the symbolic language of other poetic texts. The very designation of texts as "apocalyptic" implies that they are about "the end of the world." That final, fateful quality of apocalyptic texts is another thing that gives them such power over the human imagination. "The end of the world" arouses the hopes and fears of all the years in a way that very little else does. So, the relationship between the signs and their referents in apocalyptic texts takes on a kind of dire seriousness, much more than even Whitman's poetry about President Lincoln's death. "The end of the world" is like the trump card to end all trump cards when it comes to ascribing seriousness.

Apocalyptic texts, then, have a built-in seriousness to them because of their inescapable ramifications for all readers alike. But, of course, if apocalyptic texts truly are about "the end of the world," then it will always be the case that the referents of apocalyptic signs must be in the future. If we accept the prediction-fulfillment scheme of Left Behind Theology, Daniel's "abomination of desolation" cannot be exhausted as referring to Antiochus IV Epiphanes's act of desecrating the temple. At best, that act is a partial fulfillment of Daniel's prediction, a "foretaste" of the truly big event yet to come. Here is yet another reason why apocalyptic texts generate such power: people of faith, who want to be "Bible believing" and to "follow God's Word" like good disciples, have a built-in vulnerability to apocalyptic language. Not to be scared, convinced, or at least curious about apocalyptic texts seems to be an act of unbelief.

When we add the built-in seriousness of apocalyptic texts with the indirect referents of the symbolic language used in apocalyptic texts, it can be a pretty dangerous brew. It enables us to ascribe a kind of ultimate evil status to something with which we disagree. For pastor Fortner's sermon that I have cited above, the referent of the phrase "abomination of desolation" is clearly "apostate freewill works religion." For others, it is clearly homosexuality. For many years during the Cold War, it was clearly Communism. For early Protestants, it was virtually anything that the pope was up to, real or imagined. And so on.

It seems clear that "prophetic Daniel" used the term "abomination of desolation" to refer to Antiochus IV Epiphanes and Mark used it to refer to the Roman destruction of the temple. However, because Left Behind Theology insists on reading apocalyptic texts within a prediction-fulfillment matrix, they will only recognize these historic references as partial fulfillments of the predictions. By treating apocalyptic texts as predictions, Left Behind Theology insists that we have the task of "discerning" what the "abomination of desolation" means today, in order to "watch and be ready" for the end of the world, which is surely upon us. Personally, I think the "abomination of desolation" has something to do with those cookies that someone keeps bringing to our church functions filled with raisins pretending to be chocolate chips—but don't get me started on that!

Very few proponents of Left Behind Theology are as courageous in their attempts to read apocalyptic signs as William Miller was. At least he put a date and time to his guesses, even if he did revise it once. Others, like Hal Lindsey, seem to lack Miller's courage, even if they pretend to have the same certainty. Hal Lindsey wrote his bestselling *The Late, Great Planet Earth* in 1970.[4] And while he does not go so far as to name a date, he argued that the establishment of Israel's nationhood in 1948 meant that we were living (at that time) in the last generation. He also argued that, biblically, a "generation" is forty years. So, the indirect math of Lindsey's book suggested that the late 1980s would very likely be when the rapture and subsequent events would take place. We are now one biblical "genera-

---

4. Lindsey, *Late Great Planet Earth*.

tion" after the publication of Lindsey's book, but he continues to move forward unabated, with his ongoing Hal Lindsey Report.[5]

My fear is that if the Christian community keeps piling on guesses after guesses and then simply trudging forward when those guesses don't turn out to be true, we make our faith appear ridiculous. Already it is my sense that many people of faith and of good sense have simply given up on learning anything from the apocalyptic language of the Bible. After repeated false hope and false fears about the imminent return of Jesus, a friend of mine recently concluded, "I'd just as soon let the whackos have all of those Scriptures and read something else."

My hope is that we do not have to read something else, while leaving the second half of Daniel, the thirteenth chapter of Mark and its parallel texts in Matthew 24 and Luke 21, as well as the entirety of the book of Revelation to the whackos. It is possible to find meaningful ways for reading apocalyptic texts. One way is to reconsider what is going on when the words from the book of Daniel are repeated by Jesus in the New Testament. In what follows, we will focus on the relationship between Daniel and the Gospel according to Mark, so that we can see a more fruitful way of taking apocalyptic texts seriously without taking them literally.

Homotextuality vs. Intertextuality

As I said in chapter 3, by reading Daniel in a prediction-fulfillment matrix, Left Behind Theology offers a "homotextual" form of reading the book of Daniel, flattening Daniel's multilayered construction out into a single storyline that loses much of its richness. As an alternative, I offered a "heterotextual" way of reading Daniel that accounts for the "historic Daniel," as well as "literary Daniel" and "prophetic Daniel."

Likewise, when we see how the Gospel of Mark uses some of the same language as Daniel to describe the horrific events that are happening in a later time, Left Behind Theology continues to view the Scriptures homotextually. As stated earlier, Harold Lindsell says that Daniel's sixth-century BCE "prediction" of the "abomination of desolation" was fulfilled first in 168 BCE with Antiochus IV Epiphanes and then for a second time in 70 CE. The situation in 70 CE is what is at stake in chapter 13 of Mark.

5. Online at http://www.hallindsey.com/.

In Lindsell's reading, Mark 13 is a partial fulfillment of Daniel's words. In this homotextual reading, Mark 13 is when Jesus foresees what Daniel foresaw before him.

A better way to read the relationship between Daniel and Mark 13 is to exchange homotextuality for "intertextuality." In his book *Figuring the Sacred*, Paul Ricoeur describes intertextuality as "the work of meaning through which one text in referring to another text both displaces this other text and receives from it an extension of meaning."[6] We have already seen one example of what Ricoeur is talking about in how the plotline of the story of Joseph (Genesis 34–43) is taken and used as the outline of the story of Daniel in chapters 1–6. But, as Ricoeur says, intertextuality is never simply a retelling of the old story. As we saw, the Daniel story breaks from the Joseph story in important ways in order to demonstrate that resistance is a more faithful response to living under the empire than accommodation. When we read a Scripture intertextually, we respect the way that a later text draws from the language and meaning of an earlier text *and* we respect the way that a later text extends, modifies, or transforms the meaning of an original text, rather than merely repeating it.

I invite you to read Mark 13 this way: Mark is deliberately drawing on and reworking some previous texts from Daniel in order to say something significant about a catastrophe that was happening right before his eyes. By drawing on some of the scary, apocalyptic language of Daniel, Mark is being faithful to his biblical tradition and speaking relevantly to his own historical moment. In other words, I invite you to read the scary apocalyptic language of Mark 13 intertextually.

Mark's Intertextual Relationship with Daniel

Years after Antiochus IV Epiphanes desecrated the temple, Herod the Great rebuilt it into one of the most fascinating architectural structures of the Roman Empire. However, if you go to Jerusalem today and visit the Wailing Wall, you will be looking at all that is left of the temple that Herod the Great built. Ironically, the architectural wonder built by the authority and power of Rome was also destroyed by the authority and power of Rome. If you ask me, that is indicative of how imperial power works. If

6. Ricoeur, *Figuring the Sacred*, 148.

a temple is built as an expression of the empire's power, then the same temple can also be destroyed as an expression of the empire's power. The point is that in both magnificence and destruction the religious structure, like most religion symbols, is relegated to serving the empire. The Roman Empire demanded ultimate loyalty, and that demand casts an enormous shadow over all of the stories that we read in the New Testament.

If you go to the Roman forum today, you can see another structural expression of the Roman Empire. The Arch of Titus is a commemoration of Rome's victory over the Jewish revolt of 66–70 CE.[7] Inscribed in the Arch of Titus is a picture of victorious Roman legions carrying the seven-branched candlestick of the Jewish temple into Rome. For Rome, perhaps, this was just another stamping out of an upstart rebellion in a remote part of its empire. For Israel, it was a catastrophe, just like the tragedy of two centuries earlier when the army of Antiochus IV Epiphanes defeated them and desecrated their temple. And, of course, for those Jews (and Jewish Christians) who saw the establishment of Jerusalem and the temple as signs of God's covenant, the destruction of the temple was more than simply a military defeat. If the hope of the world rested on the promise that one day the temple would be a "house of prayer for all nations" (Mark 11:17), what does the destruction of the temple mean for the world?

It was very important, then, for Jewish and Christian people of the first century to reckon with the meaning of the destruction of the temple. And that is what Mark 13 tries to do. Even though Matthew is the first book that we encounter when leafing through the New Testament, it is important to start with the Gospel of Mark, because most New Testament scholars today accept that Mark was the first of the four Gospels to be written. Similarly, those scholars usually date it from a time that saw a Jewish rebellion against Rome, Rome's strong response of besieging the city of Jerusalem, and finally the attack that destroyed the temple. That would place the writing of Mark's Gospel somewhere in the range of 66–70 CE.

Drawing on the insights of biblical scholars, we will look at how Mark reckons with the destruction of the temple intertextually with scary, apocalyptic texts. You may want to read Mark 13 before continuing on here. (Go ahead; I'll wait.) I will not attempt to answer every possible question that might arise from reading Mark's little apocalypse, but I will

7. Crossan and Reid, *In Search of Paul*, 351–53.

invite you to consider reading the chapter the way that Mark wants it to be read.

Mark 13:1–13

Mark 13 begins with an observation and a question, which shows from the get-go that the issue in this chapter is the temple. As Jesus and his disciples are coming out of the temple, one of the disciples—whom I envision as a Gomer Pyle–type of guy who has spent his entire life in a small fishing village—looks around the temple and says, "Shazam! Would ya' looky here at these big ole stones and buildings!" The astonishment was well warranted. Any one of us might be driven to say "Shazam!" if we saw forty-foot stones and such a magnificently adorned structure.

However, Jesus' response is not quite what the disciple might have expected: "Do you see these great buildings? Not one stone will be left here upon another; all will be thrown down" (v. 2). Jesus' response moves the tone immediately from wonder to tragedy. The temple was the center of cultural life for the Jews, as well as a location fraught with political and theological significance. To say that the temple would be destroyed was to say that something catastrophic was going to happen to Jerusalem.

The disciples react to Jesus' words with the question, "when will this be and what will be the sign that all these things are about to be accomplished?" (v. 4). That question leads into the scary language that gives this chapter its reputation as an "apocalypse." The *narrative* context of Mark's apocalypse is Jesus talking about the temple, which—at that time—was still standing and inspiring awe. The *historical* context of Mark's apocalypse is that the temple has been destroyed and people of God are trying to reckon with the theological meaning of that destruction and the bombast of war that brought it on.

In Mark's day, around 66–70 CE, the burning question for anyone who put stock in the temple as the locus of God's blessings was, "Where is God in all of this destruction?" Of course, we've heard that question before—in the sixth century BCE at the time when Israel suffered defeat and so many persons (including historic Daniel) were exiled into Babylon, and in the second century BCE when Antiochus IV Epiphanes desecrated the temple. Times of extreme catastrophe typically raise questions that receive apocalyptic responses.

As we read Mark 13, Mark wants us to read it in two respects, narratively and historically. Narratively, this chapter is Jesus' response to his disciples' question about the future destruction of the temple; historically, it is Mark's response to his readers' questions about the present destruction of the temple. The signs surrounding the temple's destruction are varied. There will be false messiahs rising up and calling people to follow them (v. 6). The disciples (or the readers) will hear of war and hear the rumors of war (v. 7).[8] Nation will rise against nation; empire against empire (v. 8). The earth will reel and rock in earthquakes and famines (v. 9). Disciples (or Mark's readers) will be handed over to councils, both religious and political, because of Jesus' name, but the Holy Spirit will give them the ability to transform their persecution into an occasion for spreading the gospel (vv. 9–11). Families will be divided over what to do and will turn on one another in deadly fashion (v. 12). The conclusion to this description of calamities is, "And you will be hated by all because of my name. But the one who endures to the end will be saved" (v. 13).

There are two things that I want to point out about the initial verses in Mark 13. First, many of the descriptions that Mark includes here are reminiscent of the poetic language that we have seen in other, earlier Scripture texts. For example, the reference to earthquakes reminds us of the poetry in 2 Samuel 22 (repeated in Psalm 18), where David said the earth "reeled and rocked" during his war victories. As I pointed out in chapter 2, David's poetic description was not describing stuff that actually happened "on the ground" during David's wars. It was a poetic way of describing how God was active in the blood, sweat, and tears of the battlefield. One reason I described the earthquake of Mark 13 as "the earth will reel and rock in earthquakes" is because I am trying to make explicit that we are hearing poetic speech in Mark 13, like we heard in 2 Samuel 22 and Psalm 18.

Second, the issue that Jesus is addressing to his disciples, and that Mark is addressing to his readers, is the destruction of the temple. That is very important because Left Behind Theology has lifted so much of Mark's language (and Daniel's language) out of its original context and treated it as "destruction in general" language. Mark's text is not about airplanes being deliberately flown into the World Trade Center buildings. Mark's

---

8. The word used twice in Mark 13:7, *polemos*, is typically translated "war," but it could also be translated as "dispute" or "quarrel."

text is not about a war that might or might not be pending between Israel and Iran. Mark's text is not about the Soviet Union and the United States locked in a path of Mutually Assured Destruction. Mark's text is not about a Roman Catholic pope and his Protestant opponents. In fact, I would argue that Mark's text is not about "the end of the world" *per se*.

As frightening as many of life's awful conflicts and portents of world-changing tragedy might be, none of them is the topic at hand in Mark 13 except the destruction of the temple. The real, historic, tragic, confusing destruction of the center of Jerusalem's cultural and religious life by the Roman Empire is the topic of Mark's little apocalypse. The temple's destruction is the literary topic of Mark 13, introduced by the disciple's questions and answered by Jesus in disturbing language. And the destruction of the temple is the historical topic of Mark 13, the burning question of hope and despair facing Mark's readers around 70 CE.

I'm not saying that the *meaning* of Mark 13 is only applicable to that single moment in history when the temple was being destroyed. Certainly, what a Scripture discloses about God and God's way of being in the world can speak to any number of situations in human life. Mark recognizes that also when, in verse 9, his language turns from describing cosmic events to saying, "As for yourselves, beware." The tragedies of Mark's day had cosmic significance but also very personal dimensions.

So, one can certainly make an interpretive "application" of Mark 13 to a different historical moment than the events of 70 CE. But, it is vital to remember that the original vitriol and the deadliness of this chapter are inextricably tied to the destruction of the temple. If we draw some meaning from this text to another historical moment in life, then we ought to treat it as exactly that: an interpretive application of this text out of its original meaning to another context. We should not preface those interpretations with a simple phrase like, "the Bible says . . ." because what "the Bible says" is that this text is about the destruction of the temple. If we are using this text to talk about a current tragedy, we should use the language of "I say . . ."

Now we turn to the most compelling part of Mark's thirteenth chapter. Here we will see where Mark explicitly draws on the book of Daniel to describe the catastrophe of his day, but when we do, the text contains some very curious details that we do not want to overlook!

Mark 13:14–23

Mark 13:14 contains one of the most curious narrator moments that I know of in the Scriptures. Right in the middle of a sentence by Jesus, suddenly Mark literally interrupts the text and "takes the words right out of Jesus' mouth." Here is the sentence, and watch for the interruption: "But when you see the desolating sacrilege set up where it ought not to be (let the reader understand), then those in Judea must flee to the mountains" (Mark 13:14). Reader? What reader? The literary context of this chapter is Jesus talking to his disciples. Left Behind Theology treats these words as if Mark is specifically quoting Jesus from that moment. But, why would Jesus say anything about "the reader"?

Jesus did not say anything about "the reader." The phrase addressed to "the reader" is not coming from Jesus. It is not spoken at the temple to the disciples in response to their questions. It is an interruption of the dialogue between Jesus and his disciple by another voice coming from another time talking to other persons. The voice is Mark's, the time is 70 CE, and the other persons are Mark's readers.

Most translations of the Bible—like the NRSV I am using here—put this comment into parentheses. There are no such parentheses in the original Greek texts, but since there is such an abrupt and dramatic change in voices here, somehow and in some way, anyone translating Mark 13:14 has to communicate the voice change while making sense of the verse itself. It is a highly unusual comment, almost like the narrative equivalent of a movie where the director suddenly jumps out of his chair, runs in front of the camera, and says, "Pay attention, folks!" then sits back down, never to be seen like that again.

This curious parenthetical phase "let the reader understand" is an indicator that Mark is fully conscious of his own moment and fully conscious that his readers are trying to reckon with the destruction of the temple in 70 CE. Even while narrating a conversation between Jesus and his disciples about the "future" of the temple, set around forty years before Mark's time, Mark is thinking of the events of his time and the reader who is trying to understand it. In this brief comment, Mark explicitly demonstrates that *there is more going on here than Jesus addressing his disciples.* And the very fact that Mark feels compelled to jump out of his director's chair and to look full-faced into the camera and say, "Let the reader understand" means that there is something about this passage of Scripture that calls for the reader to exercise particular discernment. It is a unique moment of discernment, because Mark does not seem compelled to make this kind of plea anywhere else.

Isn't it curious that Mark would interrupt Jesus' words and add his own encouragement to his readers? Yes, but it is only the beginning of curiosities here. There is also a *grammatical shift* in these verses, which jumps out like a speed bump on a freeway. If we look at the verb tenses in verses 14–19 we see the future voice, framed either by the words "when you see [this], then [that] will happen" or "for in those days there will be [this] and [that]." Future, future, future. But then, in verse 20, we have Jesus saying, "And if the Lord *had* not cut short those days, no one would be saved; but for the sake of the elect, whom he *chose*, he *has* cut short those days" (my emphases).

Holy smokes! Where did these past-tense verbs suddenly come from?[9] If Jesus is truly talking to his disciples about stuff that is going to happen forty years down the road, shouldn't his language be all future tense? These curious verb changes are yet another indication that Mark is toggling back and forth between Jesus addressing his disciples and Mark addressing people in his time about their present tragedy with Jesus' words.

Between Mark inserting his voice into the middle of Jesus' words and Mark's strange change of tenses in the verbs of Jesus' words, we have two strong indicators that, while Mark 13 depicts Jesus as the one doing the talking about a future tragic event, the purpose of the text is that Mark is addressing his community about a current tragic event. Let me repeat that, because we've seen that pattern before. While it appears that Jesus is addressing his disciples about a future tragic event, Mark is using this text to address his community about an ongoing tragic event. And that place where we've seen that pattern before is in Daniel 7–12.

Remember my argument that in Daniel 7–12 the one I am calling "prophetic Daniel" is using the future-tense voice of "historic Daniel" to address his community during a present tragic event. While in the story line it appears that historic Daniel is predicting the future, all of the textual evidence suggests that these words were actually written by a much later

---

9. Special note for Greek geeks: they are aorist indicative verbs, signifying a simple past tense. Now go back to your cubicles!

person, four hundred years after the stories locate historic Daniel in the exile. That's the person I call "prophetic Daniel," the narrator whose community is trying to understand the "abomination of desolation" wrought by Antiochus IV Epiphanes in the second century BCE. Likewise, Mark is speaking to his community in 70 CE by way of Jesus' conversation with his disciples, set around 30 CE. And Mark seems to be quite open about the fact that he is doing so, by jumping up in front of the camera and saying, "Let the reader understand!"

Mark 13:24–27

The next section of Mark's Gospel begins with the kind of poetic language that we have seen elsewhere in the Scriptures—the sun darkening, the moon failing, the stars falling, and the "powers in the heavens" being shaken. We have learned that such language does not always point toward events that one would necessarily witness "on the ground." More importantly, this section is where Mark takes up Daniel's language of a "son of man coming with the clouds" and specifically connects it as the answer to the "abomination of desolation." We remember that Daniel posits "one like a son of man coming with the clouds of heaven" as an antitype of Antiochus IV Epiphanes. Antiochus IV Epiphanes was the blasphemer who illegitimately entered the temple. In response, Daniel uses the phrase "one like a son of man" to signify the legitimate one, the one who receives his dominion from the "Ancient of Days" sitting on the throne (Daniel 7:13–14).

Mark uses the phrase term "Son of Man" often. It seems that in the two centuries between when Daniel was written and when Mark was written, the phrase "one like a son of man" had come to be understood as referring to a messianic figure. Mark does not say "one like a son of man," as Daniel did. Mark particularizes this figure with the definite article. Most Bible translations try to demonstrate this particularization by capitalizing the phrase "the Son of Man." The NRSV even puts the whole phrase "the Son of Man coming in clouds" in quotation marks to help readers understand that this is a deliberate use of Daniel's earlier language. However, Mark sharpens the meaning of the term "Son of Man" before he alludes to Daniel's writings.

Significantly, "Son of Man" is the term that Jesus uses in Mark's Gospel whenever he talks about his impending trial and crucifixion. In Mark 8:31, 9:31, and 10:33, Jesus tells the disciples three times that the Son of Man is going to suffer and be killed. It is hard to say why Mark has Jesus using this third-person manner of speaking about himself in these texts. My suspicion is that Mark truly does see Jesus as the Son of Man who has received his dominion legitimately from God. But, it is important for Mark that it is precisely the suffering and crucified Jesus who has received this dominion. So, only after the three warnings to the disciples—each one using "Son of Man" specifically—do we get reference to "the Son of Man coming in clouds" in Mark 13.

Following Daniel—and actually making this connection more explicit than Daniel—Mark uses the term "Son of Man" as the answer to Rome's destruction of the temple and the subsequent diaspora of many Jews and Jewish Christians from Jerusalem. One way of reading Mark's words is that "the Son of Man coming in clouds" replaces the destroyed temple as the gathering spot for all of God's elect. In Mark 11, while driving out the moneychangers and stopping up the commerce that was happening in the temple, Jesus referred to the temple as the gathering place, "a house of prayer for all nations" (11:17). Now, in the wake of the temple's destruction and the diaspora that followed, Mark describes the Son of Man as the one who sends his angels to gather the elect from all over creation. The word that Mark uses for "gather" shares the same root as the word for "synagogue." If I may be allowed the privilege of "verbing" this noun: To a people scattered by the destruction of the temple—and disheartened by all that seemed lost in that destruction—Mark offers the hopeful vision that the crucified and risen Son of Man "synagogues" the elect.

Unlike the "pulpit fiction" of William Miller and his erroneous dating of the exact time of Jesus' return, and unlike the "pulpit fiction" of Don Fortner, who uses biblical imagery to grind his theological axe, the Gospel of Mark is not an attempt to name a specific moment of Christ's return or to use biblical images wantonly. In the face of the "abomination of desolation" desecrating the temple of his day, Mark draws on the imagery of biblical texts in order to encourage his community to hold fast to Jesus Christ, the crucified and risen Son of Man. It is a message of heroic faith. By all appearances Jesus was rejected by his own people, abandoned by his own disciples, and defeated on the cross by Rome's imperial power. Mark's message, empowered by the experience of the resurrection, proclaims that this very slain one—the Son of Man—is the one who will gather the elect in the absence of the temple. That is the message that Mark invites his community to believe, even in their present crisis of faith.

Conclusion

So, let's see if we can sew together some of the pieces that we've seen so far. In chapter 2, I pointed to the three different ways that the death of Abraham Lincoln was described: the very clinical autopsy report of Dr. J. J. Woodward, the more impassioned report of that moment by Dr. Edward Curtis in a letter to his mother, and the extremely poetic response to President Lincoln's death by Walt Whitman. Each account is quite different, but none of them is wrong by any means.

I then invited you to hear prophetic Daniel's account of his vision as a similar poetic response to the catastrophe and hope of his moment as Walt Whitman's poem. With his poetry, Whitman was able to capture the earth-shattering significance of Lincoln's death in a way that the autopsy report could not. Likewise, prophetic Daniel is not describing an event that anyone on the ground (including prophetic Daniel himself) would have seen. He is capturing the glorious and earth-shattering truth behind the events on the ground. The "one like a son of man" portrayed in the book of Daniel is a poetic promise that God is in control, despite the appearance of events on the ground.

In that same vein, the Gospel of Mark takes up the hope that Daniel expressed, and proclaims that the crucified and risen Jesus Christ is "the Son of Man coming in clouds." Mark speaks that audacious word to his community during a time when it seems that all the worship, hope, and meaning that had been invested in the temple in Jerusalem were overcome by Rome's imperial power. As such, Mark's description does not belong on a timeline, which is Left Behind Theology's version of interpreting this poetic speech like a clinical report. Mark is capturing the truth of his moment. Like prophetic Daniel from years before, Mark encourages his forlorn people to hope in the Son of Man, despite appearances.

5

Victorious Secret

A Biblical View of Naked People

BACK WHEN AL GORE was tweaking his new invention called the Internet, there were occasional glitches that made life . . . interesting. For example, once I was trying to find information on the annual meeting of the Society of Christian Ethics. Easy enough, I thought, as I typed "Society of Christian Ethics" into the empty box of a search engine. However, at the time, the ethical society must have had scruples against being online, because they had no website. (Their scruples have changed, by the way. They can now be found at http://www.scethics.org.) So, the search engine gave me a link for a phrase that it perceived to be the next best thing: a Society of Christian Nudists. (You'll have to google the nudists for yourself; I'm too embarrassed.)

My computer was posing a dilemma: Christian ethics or Christian nudists? A society built around exploring the moral contours of people of faith, or a society built around exploring the physical contours of people of faith? As the link for the Society of Christian Nudists was blinking on my computer, inviting me to experience bodies of Christ, I began to wonder about the relationship between ethics and nudity. Of course, in Sunday School I was taught that there was only one way to think ethically about nudity: Don't! Don't think about it, don't look at it, and don't even think about looking at it! And sweet old Mrs. Jansen would just spin in her grave if she knew that her Sunday School children ever tried to google nudists. It seemed like the very essence of ethics—for early teenagers anyway—was to stay as far away from nudity as possible.

But, the mere presence of this website caused me to consider the possibility of a more positive relationship between ethics and nudity. I had a nagging feeling that somewhere along the line I had heard of a form of nudity that was connected with goodness. Let's see . . . it had something to do with the "rapture" in fact. Then, it hit me. I remembered how Left Behind Theology depicted nudity positively in graphics, paintings, and clip art depictions of what the "rapture" will look like one day. The "raptured" saints were always shown as leaving this world behind with nothing but their ankles and feet exposed as they were swept headlong into the clouds of heaven. And those ankles and feet were always naked!

It seems that somewhere along the line someone decided that when the saints are "raptured" they will leave their clothes in a pile right there on the ground from where they were taken. If you ask me, these pictures are proof positive that Left Behind Theology has been infiltrated by undercover secret agents of the Society for Christian Nudists! I would make a big deal out of this, but really, it sounds rather redundant to go about trying to expose a group of nudists. So, why bother?

Or, perhaps these depictions are not the result of a conspiracy by Christian nudists. Perhaps there are other reasons to explain why the "rapture" is depicted as a nudist event. From a lovely perspective, perhaps this nudity means that those who are "raptured" are taken up and transformed into a community of heaven where nakedness is no longer an issue. It would be like a return to the primordial innocence of the Garden of Eden, where men and women are unclothed, seemingly not aware, and certainly not ashamed.

Or, from a not-so-lovely perspective, perhaps this sudden nude exodus is what initiates the seven years of "tribulation" for those who are left behind. Imagine suddenly having to deal with all of these piles of dirty clothes left in the middle of the floor. It would be like a sudden outbreak of four-year-olds all over the earth! No wonder we can expect "wars and rumors of wars." Who wouldn't be angry with all of that mess?

Well, to be honest, I don't know why Left Behind Theology depicts the "rapture" as a nude event. There is nothing inherently important about the relationship between nudity and the "rapture," as far as I can tell. But, there is indeed a relationship between ethics and nudity in the Scriptures, and it comes to pass in Matthew's description of the second coming of Christ. Of course, it has nothing to do with "raptured" saints leaving their dirty clothes behind as they saunter off into the naked paradise of heaven. In fact, the relationship between ethics and nudity in Matthew's story argues against the whole premise of Left Behind Theology. I call this depiction of nudity Matthew's "Victorious Secret." But, before we explore Matthew's view of nudity, we need some background.

Apocalyptic Language as Exposé and Protest

In the last chapter, we saw how Mark's Gospel was most likely the first of the four Gospels to appear in print, around the time of the destruction of Jerusalem in 70 CE. This destruction was such a disaster for the people of Jerusalem, as well as a hideous expression of Rome's imperial power, that Mark describes it using some of the same language that "prophetic Daniel" used to describe a similar disaster from 168 BCE. From Daniel's and Mark's use, we see that the role of apocalyptic language is to expose and decry the ugly truth of a disaster. As Walter Wink says, "Apocalyptic (unveiling) is always a protest against domination."[1]

My argument is that in 168 BCE, when Daniel describes the "one like a son of man coming with the clouds" and being given dominion and authority, he is describing the complete opposite of Antiochus IV Epiphanes. Antiochus IV Epiphanes is the arch-blasphemer, who arrogantly assumes power that does not belong to him and barges into places—like the holy place—where he doesn't belong. The "one like a son of man," on the other hand, is the one whose dominion is legitimate, because the God of heaven and earth grants it to him.

Likewise, when Rome destroys the temple in Jerusalem in 70 CE, Mark's "little apocalypse" (chapter 13) picks up on Daniel's imagery. In Mark's Gospel, this Son of Man—the legitimate one whose suffering, death, and resurrection is the means by which he exercises his dominion from God—exposes and protests the destructiveness of Rome's dominating authority. "Let the reader understand," Mark says. Receiving authority

1. Wink, *Engaging the Powers*, 103.

from God is the only valid way of having dominion; all other means are pretense. That is the exposé and protest of Mark's little apocalypse.

This conversation in Mark 13 is often called the "Olivet Discourse" by Left Behind Theology folk, because it takes place as Jesus is sitting on the Mount of Olives. Luke and Matthew also contain the Olivet Discourse, using much of Mark's apocalyptic language, but with some significant differences. It is largely in the differences that we can see how Luke and Matthew interpret where they stand in history and how they employ apocalyptic language to expose and protest the powers of their day.

Most biblical scholars theorize that when Luke and Matthew were written, they had a copy of Mark in hand, as well as some other resources that they shared and some that were unique to them. That theory begins with the easily observable fact that Luke's and Matthew's Gospels follow Mark's outline very closely. Hence, Mark, Luke, and Matthew are generally called the "Synoptic Gospels," because "syn-optic" means "to see together." This term distinguishes the Synoptic Gospels from John's very different outline and approach to his Gospel. The reason Mark is considered the most original of the three Synoptic Gospels is partly because it is the shortest and partly because hardly any stories are only found in Mark. Virtually everything Mark says is also found in Matthew and/or Luke, except for a few characteristic phrases or details. To me, this signifies that while Matthew and Luke have their own way of telling the story of Jesus Christ, they also have very high regard for the way that Mark tells the story and they follow it closely.

But, when we read the Synoptic Gospels side by side, two other things are also evident. First, Matthew and Luke share some stories between themselves that are not in Mark. For that reason, most biblical scholars believe that Matthew and Luke shared at least one source that Mark did not have. This source is usually referred to as "the Q source," or "Q" for short. There is a fairly boring and rational explanation for this name, but I like to think of Q as someone with an eye patch and a long scar, like a mysterious informer from a James Bond movie.

Second, Luke and Matthew have some stories that are unique all to themselves. Luke's source is called "L" and Matthew's source is called "M" by Bible geeks, which triples the population of mysterious informers! We can compare Luke's and Matthew's differing ways of telling the birth narrative of Jesus to see what biblical scholars mean when positing these two sources. Luke speaks of a swaddled baby in a manger, shepherds abiding in the field, and angels in the sky. Matthew speaks of an angel in a dream, magi from the east, and a child who is found living in a house (compare Luke 2 and Matthew 2). Clearly, Matthew and Luke are relying on very different sources for their information. It is in light of these easily observable characteristics that biblical scholars have hypothesized that Mark was the first Gospel written and that Matthew and Luke had Mark in hand, along with other shared (Q) and unique (L and M) resources, as they wrote.

One of the implications of this theory is that when we are reading Luke and Matthew we can ask the question, "How did Luke or Matthew tell this story similarly and differently from Mark?" We will see ways that they repeat and ways that they modify what Mark originally said. We don't ask the question, "How did Mark change Luke's or Matthew's version of this story?" because Mark did not have had Luke's and Matthew's versions on hand.

I find this approach to the Synoptic Gospels to be very helpful as a means of studying the Scriptures. If we accept that Luke and Matthew are being very intentional in the way that they write their stories, then the similarities between them and Mark mean something and the differences between them and Mark mean something. In other words, when we look at how Mark, Luke, and Matthew tell the same stories differently, we are seeing another example of intertextuality, where Matthew and Luke take up a previous text called Mark. They receive meaning from it and they modify that meaning in the retelling of the story.

For our purpose, this intertextual way of reading the Synoptic Gospels means that when we compare how Luke and Matthew talk about the scary apocalyptic matters found in the Olivet Discourse, we are looking at how Luke and Matthew repeated and modified what Mark had to say, in light of their own resources and their own theological vision. After one more piece of background information, we will look at how Luke takes up and modifies the meaning of Mark 13 in his own version of the Olivet Discourse. Then, we'll look at how Matthew does the same. It is in Matthew's unique presentation of this discourse that we hear about the relationship between ethics and nudity.

Final Piece of Background Information:
The Problem of Nothing

There is a very influential problem at hand throughout the New Testament, which becomes important when we are looking at the relationship between texts over time. That problem has been described by many biblical scholars as "delay of the *parousia*." *Parousia* is the Greek word for the noun "coming," as in "the coming of the Lord." The problem is that many texts imply that Jesus is coming back soon—either immediately or at least within the lifetime of those who were standing there in the story. This expectation of the looming *parousia* was very encouraging to those who were suffering persecution. It gave them hope that they would soon be delivered from their distress, and it was an outlook about how God was just on the verge of bringing about salvation for the world. The key is that, among most of the New Testament writers, the Lord's coming was going to happen soon and probably in their own lifetime.

However, if one text implies that Jesus is coming again immediately, and another text repeats that claim a decade or more later, then there is a problem. The later text has to account for the decade delay in some way or another, or else run the risk of people rolling their eyes and asking, "Didn't we hear that ten years ago?" That is the problem of the "delay of the *parousia*" that is addressed throughout many books of the New Testament—and the later the book, the more the problem is addressed.

The writer of 1 and 2 Peter gives the most explicit illustration of how New Testament writers struggled with proclaiming the immediacy of the Lord's coming and then dealing with the delay of the Lord's coming. I'm not sure if the writer was actually Peter the Apostle and I'm not sure if the same person wrote both letters, but let's treat these books as two letters from the same person and let's call him Peter. In his first letter, Peter makes several references to the sufferings of his audience as only lasting "for a little while." The reason that the suffering would be brief seems to be given in 1 Peter 4:7: "The end of all things is near; therefore be serious and discipline yourselves for the sake of your prayers." How comforting it must have been for those whose existence was miserable to hear that "the end of all things is near."

However, by the time 2 Peter was written there was a problem, which we could call the "problem of nothing." A whole lot of nothing happened between Peter's first and second letter—at least nothing that rises to the level of "the end of all things." Many of those who had hoped for a soon-to-come resolution to their misery were still miserable. And some people were raising questions about this problem of nothing. Peter attributes these questions to bad intentions and argues that the question itself is a sign that the last days are at hand. Second Peter 3:3–4 says, "First of all you must understand this, that in the last days scoffers will come, scoffing and indulging their own lusts and saying, 'Where is the promise of his coming [Greek: *parousia*]? For ever since our ancestors died, all things continue as they were from the beginning of creation!'"

Perhaps the folks raising the question about the delay of the *parousia* were simply being schmucks. But, even as they were scoffing and indulging in their own lusts, we should admit that the question itself had some validity. After all, 1 Peter did say that "the end of all things is near." So, a valid question would have been something like, "How near is near?"

Peter then makes this argument: "But do not ignore this one fact, beloved, that with the Lord one day is like a thousand years, and a thousand years are like one day. The Lord is not slow about his promise, as some think of slowness, but is patient with you, not wanting any to perish, but all to come to repentance" (2 Peter 3:8–9). The language that the Lord's coming was "near" in 1 Peter has now given way to the language that those who wait should be "patient" in 2 Peter. The delay, according to the Peter, is not an indication of unfaithfulness on God's part. The problem lies with the perception that God appears to be slow to those who judge by calendar time. God's time is different from calendar time.

The problem of the delay of the *parousia* might have been a problem that scoffers used to push their own wrongheaded agendas, but it also was a real problem for many sincere people in the early church. And the issues facing the early church seem to be very similar to many of the issues facing the church today.

1. It was church's consistent belief that Jesus is coming again. And it was a consistent part of the New Testament message that Jesus' second coming would be sooner rather than later. We have to say, honestly, that it would have been almost unimaginable to New Testament writers that two thousand years would pass without Jesus' coming.

2. Many of these expectations maintained that Jesus' second coming would be signified by radical events in history. The resurrection of Jesus seemed to be a huge announcement that the unusual and the miraculous was already in motion, so it was probably the first event that seemed like the harbinger of the end of all things. The destruction of the temple forty years later was more calamitous, and it also seemed to be a propitious moment for Jesus' coming because it seemed that evil had finally reached it worst point ever. And, at later moments of the nascent church's history, several of the Roman emperors were particularly nasty toward the Christian community, in ways that ramped up speculation that the end was near. The reigns of Caligula and Nero, for example, were awful and expectant times for many Christian people.

3. When "nothing" happened, faithful people faced a dilemma. While "scoffers" might have responded to the delay of the *parousia* in un-faithful ways, faithful Christians had to deal with the delay as well. Sometimes the resolution to the dilemma was to appeal to how God is not bound by the finite understanding of time that humans are—which is how 2 Peter resolves it. At other times, the resolution became more a matter of saying, "The second coming will come, but nobody knows when. So, we must always be ready." This answer is always in danger of losing its urgency after many repeated instances of getting one's hopes up only to have "nothing" happen.

4. Throughout history faithful people continue to guess, guess wrongly, hope, get disappointed, name dates, retract dates, make scary pre-dictions, retract scary predictions, and generally repeat the same patterns that one can discern within the New Testament communi-ties. Left Behind Theology in particular has made a virtual cottage industry out of ramping up expectations that Jesus is coming again any second now. But, rather than speaking these words as comfort, this message often seems to serve the purpose of capitalizing on the fears that the message conjures up. Typically, these predictions try to make the case that one's own generation is surely the most evil gen-eration ever, so that some kind of world implosion is surely bound to happen. But, let's be honest: Any old idiot can argue that the times are evil, because human community is always sinful.

Peter's way of dealing with the delay of the *parousia* is to argue for humility in our claims. Since God is above time, any so-called delay of the *parousia* is more a matter of human perception, impatience, or arrogance than an inconsistency in the Christian message or unfaithfulness on God's part. But, we should admit that Peter's argument would have been a little more convincing if he had shown that same kind of humility in the first letter, when he so confidently said that "the end of all things is near." Even adding a brief parenthetical comment like, "And when I say 'near' please understand that for the Lord a day is like a thousand years" would have been nice. But, that's not how Peter spoke about the immediacy of the Lord's coming in his first letter.

It seems to me that most Left Behind Theologians have taken Peter's inconsistency and raised it to an art form. Here's how it typically unfolds:

- First, they write tantalizing phrases like, "Every prophecy in the Bible about the second coming has now been fulfilled." Then, they point to the statehood of Israel as the lynchpin fulfillment of prophecy, placing us into the last of the last generations.

- Then, they point to the latest piece of technology as being the very thing that could end up being the mythical "mark of the beast." Once it was our ZIP code, then our phone number, then our Social Security Number, then the U.S. Postal Service's dreaded imposition of the ZIP + four digits, and now those confusing IP addresses that control our means of communication.

- Then, they point to the leaders of the League of Nations (oops, delete) the Soviet Union (oops, delete) Libya (oops, delete) Iraq (oops, delete) Afghanistan (oops, delete) Iran (yes!) as the sure embodiment of the Antichrist. If Iran has a change of heart, we can always turn back to the United Nations as the embodiment of the Antichrist.

- Then, finally, after making strong claims chock-full of social and political implications, they pull out the great caveat and say, "But no one knows the day or the hour." That way, when they're wrong—and they've all been wrong so far—they can always say, "But we didn't say that the Lord would definitely come on that date. Just that it was a very strong possibility."

I call this tactic "passive-aggressive prophesying," and I think it is detestable.

The New Testament writers believed profoundly that Jesus' life, death, and resurrection was the beginning of a new day in the world. And they wrote their books with great expectation that the new day in Christ was destined to be a globally significant event. But, at times they overstated their case. So, in time, their expectation of the *parousia* had to come to grips with their experience of too much "nothing." And they had to reappraise their understanding of how, exactly, Jesus' resurrection brings a new way of being into the world. They did not keep moving the prophetic stake farther and farther away saying, "Okay, now Jesus is coming. . . . . Darn! Okay, now! . . . Darn!" Instead they looked for other ways to embrace and express the *parousia*. And that is what we see in Luke's and Matthew's way of repeating and modifying Mark's version of the Olivet Discourse.

Luke's Version of the Olivet Discourse

We recall that it in Mark 13 we encounter the scary language about how, prior to the coming of the Son of Man, there will be wars and rumors of war, signs in the heavens, and other "apocalyptic" events. These words are all in response to a question about the destruction of the temple: "Tell us, when will this be, and what will be the sign that all these things are about to be accomplished?" (13:4). My argument has been that Mark 13 exposes and protests the Roman destruction of the temple as an illegitimate act of hubris. For Mark, Rome is arrogating for itself the kind of dominion that is rightfully given by God to the Son of Man. Of course, there is much more to the chapter, but the crisis caused by Rome's destruction of the temple is the overwhelming topic at hand.

For Luke, this immediate crisis of the destruction of the temple has passed. Of course, Rome is still Rome, but most biblical scholars would say that the destruction of the temple itself was anywhere from ten to fifteen years prior to the time Luke wrote his Gospel. With that passage of time, the urgency of the expectation that the destruction of the temple would bring about a cosmic change in the world had also waned, at least to some extent. So, when we read Luke's version of the Olivet Discourse, we will see a text that is written to a different historical moment. Luke's version still addresses a moment chock-full of Roman hubris, but it does not have the immediate crisis of the temple's destruction that animates Mark's version of the Olivet Discourse.

By holding Mark 13 and Luke 21 side by side, we can see places where Luke takes up and modifies Mark's answer to the question of when the destruction of the temple will be and what will be the signs of it. Again, for Luke, the destruction of the temple is now a historical issue, not a future prediction or a present catastrophic event.

For the most part, Luke stays rather closely to Mark's version of the Olivet Discourse—at least with regard to the flow of the conversation. To that extent, Luke affirms that Mark is representing Jesus' words fairly. But, there are differences between Mark 13 and Luke 21, which indicate different outlooks that reflect different times and different questions that Mark and Luke were facing. We will look at four of them.

First, we begin with comparing Mark 13:7 and Luke 21:9, a verse pair that pertains to the signs of the coming destruction and the persecution that will accompany them. Here is where we see the first significant difference between Mark and Luke. Mark 13:7 has Jesus saying, "When you hear of wars and rumors of wars, do not be alarmed; this must take place, *but the end is still to come.*" Luke 21:9 has Jesus saying, "When you hear of wars and insurrections, do not be terrified; for these things must take place first, *but the end will not follow immediately.*" (Emphases added.)

The Greek word *telos*, which is translated as "end" in both of these texts, can have two different shades of meaning. It can be the "end" as in the final thing in a series, like when Peter said, "The end of all things is near." Or, it can mean the goal, the endpoint toward which events are heading. Reading Mark, I get the impression that the emphasis on "the end" is to ensure that the destruction of the temple (along with much of Jerusalem and the whole center of Jewish cultural life) has a purpose and endpoint to it. To a people living in the disaster of their lifetimes, Mark records Jesus encouraging disciples to believe that the current disaster is going somewhere in God's history.

Luke, on the other hand, records Jesus telling disciples that "the end" will follow, *but not immediately.* For Luke, "the end" seems to be more explicitly temporal. It is a small difference, and one could certainly see these texts otherwise, but it is a difference that makes sense if Luke is writing fifteen years or so after the disaster at the temple occurred. The community for whom Luke is writing might well have been asking the temporal question, "Wasn't the end supposed to be here by now?" So much of biblical promise is centered around Jerusalem that even if Luke's audience was mostly Gentile, there would have been questions of this sort in the years after the temple's destruction. Luke seems to be addressing the temporal question by saying that the end is indeed coming, but Jesus did not say that it was coming *immediately*.

The second difference between Mark's and Luke's versions of the Olivet Discourse is in the next section, where Jesus is speaking about the destruction of Jerusalem. We recall Mark's cryptic parenthetical insertion "let the reader understand" as a very unique kind of narrative intrusion into Jesus' words. Luke leaves that parenthetical comment out entirely. In addition, Luke modifies the key phrase that Mark uses from "prophetic Daniel." Mark 13:14 has Jesus saying, "But when you see the desolating sacrilege set up where it ought not to be (let the reader understand), then those in Judea must flee to the mountains . . ." Luke does not speak of the desolating sacrilege, perhaps because by the time he writes the temple does not exist except as rubble. Jerusalem still exists, although in a very humbled state. So, Luke 21:20–21 has Jesus saying, "When you see Jerusalem surrounded by armies, then know that its desolation has come near. Then those in Judea must flee to the mountains . . ." Again, the verses are very similar, but the differences are meaningful.

Third, within that same section Luke makes another very obvious modification. Mark 13:20 records Jesus slipping from the future tense into the perfect tense, saying, "And if the Lord had not cut short those days, no one would be saved; but for the sake of the elect, whom he chose, he has cut short those days." It is almost as if Mark is slipping back and forth between Jesus' day (around 30 CE) and Mark's own day (70 CE). Luke does not have this comment at all. But, once again, Luke does address the issue of time. Luke 21:23–24 says something that is very unique to Luke, with no parallel in Mark's Gospel: "For there will be great distress on the earth and wrath against this people; they will fall by the edge of the sword and be taken away as captives among all nations; and Jerusalem will be trampled on by the Gentiles, until the times of the Gentiles are fulfilled."

This reference to "the times of the Gentiles" is a unique and largely unexplained phrase in Luke's Gospel. It has that kind of elusive, nobody-quite-knows-exactly-what-this-means quality to it that makes it a perfect phrase for people to "interpret" with their own meaning. But, rather than trying to map out something like "the times of the Gentiles" on a timeline of the end times, I suggest that we try to let Luke explain for himself what he means by "the times of the Gentiles."

For Luke, the resurrection of Jesus came with a commission, which is expressed in Acts 1:8 in Jesus' parting words to his disciples: "But you will receive power when the Holy Spirit has come upon you; and you will be my witnesses in Jerusalem, in all Judea and Samaria, and to the ends of the earth." The book of Acts is the ongoing story of how the church fulfills these words, by taking the story of Jesus far beyond the reaches of Jerusalem. This missionary advance was partly by design and partly by being forced out of Jerusalem by persecution. Peter has a dramatic story of going to the house of a Gentile and being astounded at how well received the gospel is there (Acts 10). But, it is Paul who makes the most inroads in his three missionary journeys, with most of his success among Gentiles. The story of Acts ends with a confrontation between Paul and a group of Jews in Rome, where Paul argues that if they refuse to listen to the gospel, somebody else will: "Let it be known to you then that this salvation of God has been sent to the Gentiles; they will listen" (Acts 28:28).

For Luke, "the times of the Gentiles" are not on a timeline somewhere, awaiting fulfillment. They are the times at hand for him as he writes his Gospel then the book of Acts. And it is an ambiguous time. The Gentiles are destructive—Roman armies surround Jerusalem. But, the Gentiles are also showing amazing receptivity to the gospel of Jesus Christ. Within that ambiguity, Luke continues to live with the expectation that Jesus' coming is near, but he interprets that nearness with respect to how he sees God at work in his own day, bringing salvation to a world filled with destructive violence.

Finally, I will suggest one last way that Luke modifies Mark's Olivet Discourse. More than the others, this modification is my own interpretation and I invite you to accept or reject it according to how you read the Scriptures. Like Mark, Luke depicts Jesus speaking of cosmic signs in the heavens that one can expect before seeing "the Son of Man coming in a cloud." Luke 21:25 says, "There will be signs in the sun, the moon, and the stars, and on the earth distress among nations confused by the roaring of the sea and the waves." Of course, these descriptions sound like foreboding words of cosmic destruction and chaos. But, I would argue, they're not. Luke does not necessarily intend these scary words to describe destruction.

Here's my argument: In the book of Acts, there is the well-known story of the Day of Pentecost, when the Holy Spirit descends on the disciples in an upper room. It is a scene of fantastic description, filled with destructive imagery—the sound of a violent wind, along with fire that falls on each disciple. But, this is not a destructive fire and the wind brings no violence. Instead, the fire represents the Holy Spirit, which gives each disciple the ability to speak in various languages about the mighty deeds of God. This fire and the sound of this windstorm mark the event where the disciples are empowered to fulfill the commission in Acts 1:8 to take the gospel to the world beyond their own language.

Following this outpouring of the Holy Spirit, a crowd gathers, bewildered at how these local yokels are able to speak about God's mighty deeds in languages from all over their known world. Some of the more jaded folk argued that they were drunk (proving that jerkification is an age-old phenomenon.) Peter stands tall and tells them that this is not drunkenness; it is a fulfillment of the words of the prophet Joel that God would pour out God's spirit in the last days. Part of this quote from Joel has the very kind of cosmic imagery that we see in Luke 21. Citing Joel, Peter says, "And I will show portents in the heaven above and signs on the earth below, blood, and fire, and smoky mist. The sun shall be turned to darkness and the moon to blood, before the coming of the Lord's great and glorious day" (Acts 2:19–20).

My argument is that the cosmic language that Luke depicts Jesus as using in Luke 21 is not the language of destruction and chaos. It is the language of God's spirit being poured out on the day of Pentecost. Of course, the sun did not really turn dark on that day. If it had, the crowd that gathered would have gone running off screaming in panic. The moon did not really turn to blood—at least, not to the extent that Luke bothers describing it that way. No, these cosmic signs are simply the language that Luke uses to describe the earth-shaking significance of what was happening on the Day of Pentecost.

Here's the point: When we read the Olivet Discourse in Luke's Gospel, it sure sounds like an awful, apocalyptic event that ushers in the second coming of Christ. Perhaps Luke's original readers are wondering when all of these celestial fireworks that they've been hearing about will take place, since the sun is still shining and the moon is still going through its ordinary phases for them. When writing the book of Acts, Luke answers that question about these celestial fireworks. The scary apocalyptic signs in the heavens from the Olivet Discourse are not literal earth-destroying phenomena. They are the same kinds of imagery that Luke uses to speak of that event when the Holy Spirit empowers Jesus' disciples to share the gospel in every language of their world, beginning in Jerusalem, and reaching out even to others. That is, Pentecost marks the beginning of "the times of the Gentiles."

What I've tried to show here is that Luke repeats much of Mark's version of the Olivet Discourse—the very part of the Gospel that seems to give Left Behind Theology all of its prophetic power. But, Luke modifies certain pieces of that discourse in order to account for how he understands the coming of Jesus. For Luke, the scary apocalyptic language is all part of this magnificent activity that God is doing in the world through Spirit-empowered disciples. They are taking the gospel to Jerusalem and beyond, even to the Gentiles. Not global destruction, but great missionary activity is, for Luke, the essence of what the apocalyptic imagery of the Olivet Discourse is all about.

Matthew and Naked People

Like Luke, Matthew also had a copy of Mark's Olivet Discourse in hand. And like Luke, Matthew repeats some of that discourse and modifies some of it. In fact, Matthew makes one enormous modification of the Olivet Discourse, which allows us to see how Matthew is answering the problem of "the delay of the *parousia*." And that is where nakedness comes in.

In Matthew 24, Matthew follows Mark's outline of the Olivet Discourse closely. Like Mark and Luke, Jesus talks about the destruction of the temple, the signs of the times, the fate of Jerusalem, the coming of the Son of Man, the lesson of the fig tree, and an encouragement to keep awake and watch. But, whereas Mark and Luke end the discourse with this encouragement and move back to their narrative describing the plot to kill Jesus, Matthew's Olivet Discourse keeps going. A lot. It includes a warning about faithful versus unfaithful slaves in chapter 24, then keeps on going in chapter 25 with a parable about ten bridesmaids, a parable about talents, and the concluding story of the judgment of the nations. In the end, Matthew's Olivet Discourse is more than twice as long as Mark's or Luke's. And there is nothing—absolutely nothing—in the literary construction of Matthew 24 and 25 that suggests any breaks in the story. For Matthew, these two chapters are one, long, unbroken discourse.

That bears repeating, because it is so pivotal: For Matthew, chapters 24 and 25 are one, long, unbroken discourse. Even the segue between chapters 24 and 25 is a random break, because the text itself does not indicate the end of one conversation and the beginning of another. In fact, 25:1 begins with the connective word "then." No doubt about it, Matthew 24–25 constitutes one, long, unbroken Olivet Discourse.

So, two questions arise: First, why am I making such a big hairy deal out of this one, long, unbroken discourse? Second, what does it matter that Matthew 24–25 constitutes one long, unbroken discourse?

Excellent questions; thanks for asking. I'll try to answer both of these questions together. When Matthew takes Mark's Olivet Discourse and more than doubles it, we have a very clear literary indicator that Matthew is addressing something that seems unresolved by Mark's version of this discourse. Matthew is not content to simply restate Mark's version of the Olivet Discourse, so one way of taking Matthew's intentions seriously is to recognize how he modifies Mark and to explore why. I suggest that the key to understanding what Matthew is up to is found in the last part of Matthew's discourse, the story of the judgment of the nations (25:31–46), which begins with the words, "When the Son of Man comes in his glory, and all the angels with him, then he will sit on the throne of his glory." Take note that the "Son of Man," which is a term that depicts the suffering servant of God, is now a king, sitting on a throne. We'll see that paradoxical imagery again from the book of Revelation in the next chapter.

In this concluding story to his Olivet Discourse, Matthew is going to show what it will look like when the Son of Man comes in all of his glory. The nations of the world line up and are separated, like sheep and goats. The "sheep" on his right hear the invitation, "Come, you that are blessed by my Father, inherit the kingdom prepared for you from the foundation of the world . . ." (v. 34). The "goats" on his left hear the Son of Man utter the awful words, "You that are accursed, depart from me into the eternal fire prepared for the devil and his angels . . ." (v. 41). So far, this is a very typical depiction of the final judgment, which people of many different religions are wont to imagine—"us" versus "them," "the good" versus "the evil," "the chosen" versus "the great unwashed." But Matthew's story does not follow the typical plotline. In fact, Matthew very deliberately turns this plotline inside out.

The great surprise of this story is that neither the sheep nor the goats quite understand why they have been designated as sheep or goats. To the sheep, the Son of Man tells them why they are invited into the kingdom: "For I was hungry and you gave me food, I was thirsty and you gave me something to drink, I was a stranger and you welcomed me, I was naked and you gave me clothing, I was sick and you took care of me, I was in prison and you visited me" (vv. 35–36). For the goats, they are condemned because they treated the Son of Man in just the opposite way: "for I was hungry and you gave me no food, I was thirsty and you gave me nothing to drink, I was a stranger and you did not welcome me, naked and you did not give me clothing, sick and in prison and you did not visit me" (vv. 42–43).

Both the sheep and the goats have the same reaction to this explanation of why some of them are blessed and some are condemned. Each of them ask, "Lord, when was it that we saw you hungry and gave you food, or thirsty and gave you something to drink? And when was it that we saw you a stranger and welcomed you, or naked and gave you clothing? And when was it that we saw you sick or in prison and visited you?" (vv. 37–39 and again in shortened form in v. 44). Both groups ask! The difference between sheep and goats is not that one of them has insider knowledge and the other does not—they're both confused. "We did what? When?"

So far, Matthew has completely ruined our expectations about the final judgment. I know of no other depiction of the final judgment in any literature where the shared experience of both the glorified and the condemned is confusion. What a unique story!

But, the best is yet to come. The Son of Man's answer to the question, "Lord, when did we see you hungry, etc.?" is the most astounding part of the whole Olivet Discourse in Matthew (in my humble opinion). To the confused sheep, the Son of Man answers, "Truly I tell you, just as you did it to one of the least of these who are members of my family, you did it to me" (v. 40). Likewise, the Son of Man says that the goats failed to offer him food, etc. when they did not do so for "the least of these" (v. 45). The word "least" here is not a put down; it refers to quantity, like "a single one."

In other words, Matthew's one, long, unbroken discourse answers the question of the return of the Son of Man profoundly. Long before the final judgment, the Son of Man returns repeatedly in the guise of the hungry, the thirsty, the stranger, the naked, the sick, and the imprisoned. That is how Matthew answers the problem of "the delay of the *parousia*." The *parousia* is not "delayed"; it is happening right now, beneath our noses, whenever a single one of God's children is found in need.

And that is the biblical view of naked people. Naked people—biblically speaking—are those who are in need, who do not have the basic clothing that they need for warmth and well-being. It is when we encounter naked people and offer them the clothing they lack that we are actually reaching out and embracing the Son of Man who has returned. Matthew argues that we do not need to look upwards at the heavens to see the coming of the Son of Man. To see the Son of Man, we look downward at those humbled persons among us who are languishing in need. Matthew's "Victorious Secret" is this: "Look to the naked and you will see the return of the Son of Man."

6

I'll Be Back

The Return of Jesus' Evil Twin

IT SEEMED LIKE A common enough statement. A group of pastors were gathered around the table, discussing biblical texts for the upcoming season of Advent. The word "Advent" is from the Latin word that means "coming," and it is the name that is given to the four Sundays prior to Christmas on the Christian liturgical calendar. During those Sundays, many Christian churches turn their attention to various readings from the Hebrew Bible that express how the people of Israel were longing for a coming Messiah. By reading those texts, churches try to share that longing with the people of old, in order to appreciate the wonder of the Christmas story more pointedly. But, the season of Advent has a double meaning. It is more than just reliving the anticipation of the first coming of Jesus. It is also a way of focusing on being faithful now, in our time, as we await the second coming of Jesus.

And so, the group of pastors were looking at some of the biblical texts that are often read during this season and were talking about what it means to live in the "in-between times" of the first and second coming of Christ. Then one pastor said, "Well, you know that the first time Jesus came, he came like a Lamb; but, the next time he comes, he is coming like a Lion!" It was not a new idea, by any means, but there was something in the way that this pastor made this comparison between the first and second comings of Jesus that caused me to see—for the first time—just how weird this assumption is.

Thinking Theologically about Biblical Texts

The assumption that Jesus' first and second comings will be as antithetical as the metaphors of a Lamb and a Lion is truly astounding. That means that everything we know about Jesus from the Gospels of the New Testament (Matthew, Mark, Luke, and John) is going to be different when Jesus returns a second time—his personality, his message, his activities, and especially his way of being the Messiah who brings a message of salvation for the world. The two different ways that Jesus comes look like this.

(Cue background music to the "Barney" song.) The first time Jesus came, he was nice, like a Lamb. He loved people. He ate with outcasts. He met violence by turning the other cheek. He even prayed that God would forgive his tormentors. Okay, there was that incident of cleansing the temple that got a little raucous, but it was for a good cause. And, most important of all, Jesus brought us salvation by willingly taking that awful journey to Jerusalem and enduring the cross and its shame. In fact, many people look to this writing from Isaiah to describe Jesus' death: "He was oppressed, and he was afflicted, yet he did not open his mouth; like a lamb that is led to the slaughter, and like a sheep that before its shearers is silent, so he did not open his mouth" (Isaiah 53:7). This is the coming of Jesus "as a Lamb," to use my colleague's phrase. But, as my colleague goes on to argue, this nice "Jesus as a Lamb" was not the end of the story.

(Switch background music to Beethoven's Fifth Symphony.) Alas, the world continues to be a dark and stormy place. While Jesus' first attempt at being Messiah—"as a Lamb"—might be enough to forgive our sins at a very personal level, it obviously has failed at bringing salvation and transformation to the world. So, the next time Jesus comes, we will see a very different side of him. This time around, Jesus is no longer a Lamb, trying to overcome evil with good. Nope, that Lamb stuff has fallen by the wayside, like a child who grows up and drops all of the idealism of his youth. This Jesus of the second coming is a Lion—a teeth-baring, clawed up, growling "Lion of Judah" who knows exactly how to deal with evildoers. He's come a long way from his idyllic days when he said things like, "Father, forgive them." Now he says things like, "You had your chance. Now it's too late!"

What follows is a bloodbath, with Jesus sending foot soldiers and generals and all kinds of heavenly armies to wreak havoc.

This extreme contrast between Jesus' first coming and his second coming is very widely accepted today, partly because many people feel that this is precisely what the Scriptures describe. But, before looking at the Scriptures involved, isn't it worth asking what these two descriptions say about Jesus himself? That would be a question of "Christology." And, since one way of describing Jesus is that he reveals God and God's reign to us, isn't it worth asking what these Lamb-then-Lion descriptions say about God? That would be a question of "theology." If we lay these descriptions side by side, even if we just take the metaphors of Lamb and Lion and hold them together, there are substantial differences in what they say about Jesus and, consequently, about God. In fact, if we accept the Lamb-then-Lion descriptions, I see them leading to three options, none of which seems very promising.

First, we could simply conclude that Jesus is bipolar. Bipolarity is not funny and I am not taking it lightly, but it is at least one way of explaining how someone can be as peace-loving as Gandhi one moment, and as warlike as Napoleon the next. Of course, none of us wants to take this option, because it simply seems heretical to say that Jesus is mentally ill. But, if we ever were to describe any other person in the Lamb-then-Lion scheme that we use so commonly for Jesus, bipolarity would certainly have to be one option for imagining how one and the same person could contain such contrasting personalities.

The second option is that perhaps one of these two personalities is not Jesus' true personality. And, in fact, if we accept everything that Left Behind Theology has to say about Jesus—and the God whom Jesus reveals to us—then the Lamb Jesus is not Jesus' true personality. Jesus' Lamb-like personality was a thirty-three year experiment that failed. As an experiment, the Jesus of loving enemies and turning the other cheek was not the essence of who Jesus truly is. It was his chivalrous, but ultimately futile attempt to overcome evil with good. Perhaps Jesus knew all along that it would fail and that he would eventually have to return with guns ablazin' before it was all over. My point is this: If what Left Behind Theology says about the second coming of Jesus and his way of dealing with evil is accurate, then Jesus and his way of dealing with evil in his first coming was not his true personality. It was a well-meaning attempt to make nice that failed.

You might be thinking, "But, wait, maybe the difference between the first and second coming is not in Jesus' personality. Maybe the world has just become so evil that 'Jesus as Lion' is the only option left!" That is an interesting thought, and Left Behind Theology invests a lot of effort in demonstrating to us that the world is getting more and more evil every day. But, the presence of evil and rebellion against the reign of God are nothing new in the world. In fact, first-century Judea—where Jesus' Lamb personality was his way of proclaiming God's message—was a violence-filled place, dominated by the imperial rule of Rome. Besides, if Jesus' leonine second coming is supposed to have been predicted by the historic Daniel, then it would appear that God has been planning on the "Lion option" since at least the sixth century BCE. If that were the case, then Jesus' philosophy of "overcoming evil with good" was not only a failure, it was a ruse. God knew better all along.

For my money, the first two options for explaining the extreme difference between the Lamb Jesus in his first coming and the Lion Jesus in his second coming are not convincing. It seems irreverent to think of Jesus has having a mental illness, although many good people do suffer from such. And, it seems equally irreverent to suggest that the Lamb Jesus was not Jesus' true personality. So, that leads us to the third option, which is this: The Lamb is really Jesus, but the Lion is his evil twin, Ahnold.

Think about it! The Lamb is Jesus Christ; the Lion is Ahnold Christ. Everything that Jesus was about, Ahnold is trying to tear down. Jesus says, "turn the other cheek because good triumphs over evil"; Ahnold says, "Strike the other's cheek!" Jesus says, "Love your enemies"; Ahnold says, "Your enemies are God's enemies. Kill them in the name of heaven!" Jesus says, "Blessed are the peacemakers"; Ahnold lets loose four horsemen on the earth, whose noble steeds are named "Pestilence, War, Famine, and Death." Jesus dies on the cross, obediently yielding himself to his enemies; Ahnold willingly accepts God's new directive to annihilate the enemies (along with most of God's creation). In Jesus we see that, even in rejection, God's steadfast love endures forever; in Ahnold we see that God's steadfast love is on a timer and we are nearing the midnight hour when it's over. I'm telling you, there is something to the idea that this Lion of the second coming is Jesus' evil twin Ahnold, if the scenarios that we consistently hear from Left Behind Theology are true.

That's right: *if* the scenarios that we hear from Left Behind Theology are true. The problem is, they're not true. Jesus is not bipolar; Jesus was not putting on a ruse when he only seemed to be a Lamb for thirty-three years; everything that Jesus was about will not be unraveled by his evil twin Ahnold, the Lion of the second coming. We most assuredly can believe that God's steadfast love really does endure forever. So, as much as the scary, apocalyptic portions of the Bible seem to be glorifying violence and following the worn-out Hollywood doctrine that peace only comes by means of a bloodbath, we can think otherwise.

For those of us whose understanding of Jesus Christ has been shaped by the Gospels, the premise that Christ is only able to save the world by destroying most of it is simply wrong. And, for those of us whose understanding of God has been shaped most expressly by Jesus Christ, the idea that God will only renew creation by following some kind of Hollywood "shoot 'em up" story line is not the story about our God, but about some hideous pretender. And that, my friends, is the true purpose of those scary end-time Scriptures: distinguishing the loving God from the hideous (yet believable) pretender.

The violent, vengeful God made known to us in Ahnold Christ is the hideous, yet believable pretender. Whatever else we might say about the violence that is certainly in the book of Revelation, or the threatening tone that is certainly in the apocalyptic texts in Daniel and the Gospels, we must say this: The God who is made known to us in Jesus Christ is not the God whose way of salvation is accomplished through vengeful violence. In fact, the cross is the primary symbol that God's way of salvation is the antithesis of vengeful violence. Any God whose way of salvation is accomplished through vengeful violence—and there are plenty—is the hideous pretender.

There is a way to keep the pretender, whose way is made known in the destructive violence of Ahnold Christ, distinct from the God whose way of salvation is made known to us in the life, death, and resurrection of Jesus Christ. The key lies in how we read the Scriptures. If we read them homotextually—as flattened out, one-directional stories in a prediction-fulfillment matrix—then we get the impression that Ahnold Christ, the destroying avenger, is the Promised One. As the Left Behind Theology story tells it, Daniel predicted that Jesus would come not as a Lamb but as a Lion. In this reading of Daniel, the Promised One is coming as Ahnold Christ, the avenger. And although it appears that the Lamb-like Jesus did not come in that way, Left Behind Theology tells us that Jesus echoed Daniel's sentiments when he said that he would come back as Ahnold Christ, the Lion. And, as Left Behind Theology concludes, the book of Revelation shows that, in fact, Jesus will come back as Ahnold Christ. A homotextual reading of the Scriptures makes the Lamb-like Jesus-we-know-from-the-Gospels a minor and vanishing part of the overall Jesus story. Ahnold is the point.

Contrary to the homotextual, prediction-fulfillment scheme of Left Behind Theology, I want to offer this simple key for interpreting Scriptures that speak about the future: Instead of letting the "Lion King" Jesus of Left Behind Theology imagination shape the way we read the Gospels, we should let the Jesus whom we meet in the Gospels determine the way that we understand the Jesus of the second coming. What I mean is that we should not treat the Lamb Jesus as if he were a thirty-three year experiment with niceness that failed. Rather, we should accept that the life, death, teachings, and resurrection of Jesus are indeed who Jesus is, and anything we might say about Jesus' second coming must be understood as this Jesus—the Jesus of the Gospels—and no other.

To do that, however, we need to articulate a way to read the Lamb and Lion texts with consistent seriousness. A simplistic reading ends up with two contrasting personalities that cannot be reconciled in one person. A better reading would be to see the Lamb and the Lion as fully representing one and the same Messiah. And the means of reading these two metaphors together is given powerfully in the book of Revelation.

Coming to Terms with the Book of Revelation

You may be thinking that the book of Revelation is simply a "Jesus as Lion" book through and through. Even for the casual reader, Revelation is filled with violent imagery and its language of the Lion seems to depict Jesus as an angry, Ahnold-like avenger. Certainly a non-casual reader like Martin Luther saw Revelation as being a problematic book. Finding it to be "neither apostolic nor prophetic," Luther's final argument for rejecting Revelation is this: "For me this is reason enough not to think highly of it:

Christ is neither taught nor known in it. But to teach Christ, this is the thing which an apostle is bound above all else to do; as Christ says in Acts 1, 'You shall be my witnesses.' Therefore I stick to the books which present Christ to me clearly and purely."[1]

Few people today feel as free as Luther did to accept or reject the authority of a biblical book, but by no means was Luther alone in questioning the ongoing relevance of the book of Revelation in church history. In some of the early Christian communities of the East, the New Testament did not contain the book of Revelation (or 1 and 2 John, 2 Peter, or Jude). Revelation was also excluded from the Bible in 692 by the council of Constantinople.[2] On the other hand, many others in the church's history have found Revelation to be enormously meaningful. But, even among those who accepted Revelation as sacred Scripture, there were immense differences in how it was to be read and interpreted.

Today there continue to be those within the church who find considerable meaning in the book of Revelation and there continue to be those who struggle with its meaning and relevance. Partly this struggle is due to all of the symbolism, the meanings of which may be lost to those of us who are separated from John's world by two millennia. Partly this struggle is due to the enormous amount of violence in the book of Revelation. To me, the violence is the more difficult issue at hand when reading the book of Revelation.

Folks who are living in contexts of oppression find substantial meaning in the violent imagery of the book of Revelation. The blood-washed martyrs asking, "Sovereign Lord, holy and true, how long will it be before you judge and avenge our blood on the inhabitants of the earth?" (Revelation 6:10) is a tremendously apt depiction of the frustration that oppressed peoples often feel in the firestorm of their experience. For many victims, the violence in the book of Revelation is what makes it "real." This book is not a story of La-La Land, where being a person of faith means that life will always be beautiful and glorious. That kind of story would simply not ring true for too many people throughout human history.

Some critics of the book of Revelation feel that it glorifies violence by depicting it as God's means of bringing salvation to the world. While the book of Revelation can certainly be interpreted that way, I would encour-

1. *Luther's Works*, 35:395–99.
2. Soulen, *Sacred Scripture*.

age you to see the violence of Revelation as its mark of realism in an often violence-filled world. The violence is the context of—not the resolution to—the problem in Revelation. With that perspective, Revelation can be a powerful witness to God's salvation at work, even in a world that is steeped in hideous violence. That is quite different from saying that God accomplishes salvation in the world by means of hideous violence.

It is important to say aloud that a literal, play-by-play reading of the book of Revelation is not the way that many faithful folk throughout the history of the church have read this book. There are, and always have been, other ways of reading the book of Revelation that take it seriously without taking it literally. I would like to offer one of them here. What I will not do here is give a chapter-by-chapter commentary on Revelation. There are plenty of good commentaries on Revelation out there that are well researched and faithfully written and are not of the Left Behind Theology type. (See those by Metzger, Schüssler Fiorenza, Collins, and especially Rossing listed in the bibliography.) What I am offering is more of a starting point, a way of letting the book of Revelation itself provide us with a strategy for reading. And that strategy is given using the metaphors of the Lamb and the Lion.

When the Lion Is the Lamb

A truly stunning moment of the book of Revelation is in the fifth chapter, where John the revealer looks to see a mighty warrior king, and gets a surprise. Here's the situation: In the fourth chapter, John has been brought up through a door into heaven to see what must take place. There he sees "one on the throne," surrounded by twenty-four elders and some weird creatures all of whom are described very poetically. It is a glorious scene and all of these heavenly creatures worship the one who is on the throne. In the fifth chapter, John sees that there is a scroll in the hand of the one on the throne. It seems clear to John that the scroll contains information that affects the fate of the world, but the scroll is sealed up with seven seals. A loud voice asks, "Who is worthy to open the seals?" and in all of heaven not one single being is found worthy. So, John begins to weep. But, one of the elders turns to John and encourages him, saying, "Do not weep. See, the Lion of the tribe of Judah, the Root of David, has conquered, so that he can open the scroll and its seven seals" (Revelation 5:5). So, John turns to see the Lion, the one who has conquered, who alone is worthy to open the scroll.

At this point, the reading has us perched on the edge of our seats to see what this Lion of Judah is like. For John's community, as well as anyone who has read the Gospels, we know who the Lion is. The title "the Root of David" is a consistent way that the Gospels describe Jesus, in order to interpret his life and ministry through the imagery of Isaiah 11:1–11 and Jeremiah 23:5–6. This imagery promises that from the Davidic line— which appeared to be dead at the time—God will raise up a righteous king who will rule the nations with justice. So, we know who the Lion is. What we don't know is what he will be like. The metaphor of Lion carries with it images of vicious strength. It must be Ahnold, right?

Before we return to the narrative, let me make two other observations about this Lion about to be revealed. First, the elder says that the Lion of the tribe of Judah has *already* conquered. The verb that the elder uses to describe the Lion is a simple past-tense form that typically describes a completed action. It is terribly significant that the elder describes the Lion to John as one who has already conquered. Whatever the scroll says, whatever happens as each seal is broken, the question at hand is not "Will the Lion conquer?," "Who will the Lion conquer?," or "How will the Lion conquer?" Those questions are moot; the Lion has already conquered. By chapter 5 of Revelation, the Lion has already conquered. What follows is not the conquering itself. It is something else because the conquering has already happened.

Second, the scene does not only allude to the imagery of Isaiah and Jeremiah, who speak of the coming King from the lineage of David. It also is a reprisal of the scene that we've already witnessed in Daniel 7:13–14, which also takes place around a glorious throne: "As I watched the night visions I saw one like a [son of man] coming with the clouds of heaven. And he came to the Ancient One and was presented before him. To him was given dominion and glory and kingship, that all peoples, nations, and languages should serve him. His dominion is an everlasting dominion that shall not pass away, and his kingship is one that shall never be destroyed."

Revelation 4–5 is another instance of intertextuality, where John is taking an earlier text, the heavenly scene from Daniel 7, and is both receiving meaning from it and extending its meaning. It is the same heavenly scenario, the same honored one sitting on the throne, and the same act of legitimation that is going on in Daniel 7 and Revelation 4–5. In Daniel, the "one like a son of man" was the legitimate recipient of dominion, not the loud beast who was trumpeting arrogant words. In Revelation, the question of legitimation has to do with who is worthy to open the scroll that the enthroned one has in his hands. The answer is that the Lion is worthy to open the scroll—not because of what he is about to accomplish, but because he already has conquered.

And so we turn back to the scene as John is describing it. John looks to see this Lion of Judah. With a name like "Lion of Judah," its gotta be Ahnold, right? Here is what John sees:

> Then I saw between the throne and the four living creatures and among the elders *a Lamb standing as if it had been slaughtered,* having seven horns and seven eyes, which are the seven spirits of God sent out into all the earth. He went and took the scroll from the right hand of the one who was seated on the throne. When he had taken the scroll, the four living creatures and the twenty-four elders fell before the Lamb, each holding a harp and golden bowls full of incense, which are the prayers of the saints. They sing a new song: "You are worthy to take the scroll and to open its seals, for you were slaughtered and by your blood you ransomed for God saints from every tribe and language and people and nation; you have made them to be a kingdom and priests serving our God, and they will reign on earth." (Revelation 5:6–10, my emphasis)

While there are many fascinating pieces to this vision, what we need to note for now is that the Lion *is* the Lamb. Contrary to Left Behind Theology, for whom the Lamb is a vanishing point in the story of Jesus, the book of Revelation argues that the everything we look for in the Lion—the conquering one who alone is able to open the scroll of the world's fate—is found in the Lamb. And, in case we miss the power of this moment, it is "a Lamb, standing as if it had been slaughtered," whose conquering is described with reference to that bloodshed: "you were slaughtered and by your blood you ransomed for God saints from every tribe and language and people and nation . . ."

So here is the point: If you want to know what a conquering Lion looks like in the book of Revelation, there is no better place to look than the Gospels. The Lion in Revelation is not an alternative to the Lamb of the Gospels. They are one and the same. In fact, if one of the metaphors has priority over the other, it is that whatever we are expecting in a Lion of Judah has already been fulfilled in the Lamb of Jesus, who "has conquered" by his suffering death.

The enigma, that the Lion *is* the Lamb, is a key for reading the book of Revelation. In many ways, it is the "revelation" itself. This is not a book that breaks completely from the storyline of the Gospels. Nor is it a kind of grand finale when the Lion Ahnold comes breaking out of his disguise as the Lamb Jesus. Instead, the book of Revelation itself invites us to see the world differently, as a world where everything we long for in the conquering Lion is already accomplished in the slaughtered Lamb. It is an enigmatic vision of the world that completely turns our expectations upside-down. The Lamb Jesus of the Sermon on the Mount calling his disciples to turn the other cheek; the Lamb Jesus who asks a drink from the woman at the well; the Lamb Jesus who touches unclean lepers and dead bodies; the Lamb Jesus who is betrayed, arrested, tortured, and crucified; this Jesus *is* the conquering Lion who alone is worthy to open the scroll. You could say that the world as we know it ends when it turns out that the Lion is the Lamb.

That is the key to the book of Revelation. When what we expect in the conqueror Lion is revealed in the slaughtered Lamb, the world as we know it has come to an end. Whatever follows—no matter how bloody and violent, no matter how boastful or frightening—whatever follows this revelation is forever changed by it. The Lion is the Lamb. Whoever asserts to be the Lion in a way other than the slaughtered Lamb is the great pretender, whether his name is Ahnold, Caesar, or even a pretentious Christian who purports to be engaging in Holy War in the name of God.

As I said above, it is not my intention to address every metaphor or symbol or action in the book of Revelation and to say, "this means that and that means this." My intention is to offer a way of reading the book of Revelation and, particularly, to honor John's own indicator of how to read it. We read the book of Revelation through the enigma that the conquering Lion is in fact the slaughtered Lamb.

Revelation as a "Legitimation" Story

I have used the term "legitimation" to describe the scenarios in Daniel 7 and in Revelation 4–5 several times. I am using that term in a very specific way, and for a very specific purpose. During the era of the early church, there was every reason to question the legitimacy of saying, "Jesus is Lord." First of all, the phrase "*so-and-so* is Lord" had already been in use for some time, particularly since the time of Caesar Augustus, the first undisputed emperor of the Roman Empire. Caesar Augustus was called many things by his worshippers—Son of God, Divine One, God from God, Lord, Liberator, Redeemer, and Savior of the World[3]—and he had the battlefield narratives to prove it. Through statues, base reliefs, frescoes, and other means of art, the message throughout the Roman Empire was that Caesar's battlefield exploits were proof positive that he was chosen and blessed by the gods. In other words, it was common thinking that one's exploits on the battlefield were signs of divine favor. Since that was the case, Caesar Augustus—with many of the Caesars that preceded and followed him—was regarded in divine terms.

To say "Caesar Augustus is Lord" made sense from the common way of thinking, which accepted imperial power as normal. If an elder had said, "Caesar has conquered," it would not have been a startling statement. But, to say that one who was betrayed, arrested, tortured, crucified, and buried is "Lord" was remarkable. Even before the early Christians got to the good part—that Jesus was raised by God into new life—a typical response would have been, "Wait! You lost me at 'crucified.' How can one who is crucified be Lord?" It didn't make sense to the thinking of people throughout the empire. That is why the Apostle Paul says that the preaching of "Christ crucified" is "foolishness to the Gentiles" (1 Corinthians 1:23). The typical "wisdom" of the age was that one's divine favor was proven on the battlefield.

There is a wonderful scene from the movie *Life of Brian* where the fictitious "People's Front of Judea" are having a clandestine meeting to rail against the Roman Empire. The leader asks the rhetorical question, "What has Rome ever done for us?" To his chagrin, someone actually raises his hand and says, "The aqueduct?" After grudging acceptance, someone else added, "Sanitation." The list grew on and on while the question became, "Yes, but besides all that, what *else* has Rome ever done for us?" It is a smart scene—as most Monty Python scenes are—because the Roman Empire was not just a brutal oppressor of the nations. The empire brought a mixture of religion, violence, propaganda, as well as changes that did bring many genuinely positive effects for those who were compliant to its

3. Borg and Crossan, *First Paul*, 121.

rule. And Rome worked hard to convince its defeated nations that they were now part of something divinely ordained, an order established by the gods to bring peace on earth.

Part of what distinguishes the Roman Empire from empires before and after is how effectively their propaganda blended their military prowess with the message that Rome was ordained by the gods to bring peace on earth. In many places there were sculptures that reminded people about the benefits of complying with Rome and about what happens when a country resists Rome. The Arch of Titus and its depiction of the valuables that were taken from the temple in Jerusalem is but one example. In other places there were "Roman roads" that made military movements more practical for Rome's sake, but also had the added benefit of making commerce more practical for local peoples. In other places there were artworks and temples and enormous coliseums dedicated to local gods, as well as the Roman pantheon. And in many parts of the empire there was a form of peace, the famous *Pax Romana*, which began with Caesar Augustus and held more or less for roughly two hundred years.

To be sure, the Roman Empire was a "domination system," heavily predicated on the power of the Roman military. But, it was not simply an exercise of brute force. The Romans embedded their violence within a theology of the gods' favor and within a political promise of peace. It was, to use Marcus J. Borg's and John Dominic Crossan's scheme, a way of peace that was attained through violence and ordained by religion. Borg and Crossan sketch out the Roman way of peace this way:

Religion >>> Violence >>> Victory >>> Peace

Against that, Borg and Crossan argue that Paul—and I would add John the Revelator, if we read him correctly—proclaimed in Christ a different way toward peace:

Religion >>> Nonviolence >>> Justice >>> Peace[4]

While the competing claims of Christianity and Rome both end up hailing peace as their final goal, the grist of their differences lie in the means toward that end. For Rome, it was exactly the Lion-like Ahnold figure—the battlefield victor—who was proclaimed divine Lord and Savior. For John, it was by means of his suffering death that the Lion/

4. Ibid.

Lamb had already conquered. In other words, it is precisely the imperial relationship between theology and vengeful violence that the book of Revelation subverts. And that points to the most troubling aspect of Left Behind Theology. By depicting Jesus' second coming as Ahnold the Lion, Left Behind Theology is more akin to the theology of the Roman imperial system than it is to the Christian message.

Walter Wink has given memorable and apt names to the kind of legitimation story that Rome preached throughout its empire, and the proclamation that early Christians preached as a counter-story throughout the empire. The Roman story was what Wink calls the "Myth of Redemptive Violence."[5] It is a familiar mythology that continues to be the plotline today in television dramas, cloak-and-dagger novels, action films, video games, and even much of that curious genre of so-called Christian fiction. The idea is that redemption comes by means of "good violence," enacted by a hero whose motives set him (almost always a him) apart from the evil one, even if his actions are curiously similar. In the end, the hero wins because the gods, fate, or the scriptwriters always ensure that he has one more bullet in his arsenal than the evil one. But, the point is that no matter how nasty the violence gets (the more violence the better, if the story is aimed at teenage boys!), good always wins out in the end. This plotline is virtually identical to the legitimation story of the Roman Empire.

Contrary to that mythology is what Wink calls the "Myth of Redemptive Suffering." Here is the story that appears to be so foolish to the Gentiles in the Apostle Paul's words and the message that is dismissed as hopeless naïveté in what we often call today the "real world." And, I would argue, if we read the drama of the book of Revelation through the startling enigmatic revelation that the Lion is the Lamb, then we begin to see that the Myth of Redemptive Suffering is the storyline there as well. For example, look at how suffering becomes the means of conquering in Revelation 12:7–12. The story there is fraught with the violent imagery of war, where "Michael and his angels" fight against the dragon and his angels in heaven and defeat them. The dragon—who is called the Devil and Satan and is the deceiver of the whole world—is thrown down out of heaven. He has been conquered and a loud voice proclaims the defeat in these words:

5. Wink, *Engaging the Powers*, 13ff.

Now have come the salvation and the power and the kingdom of our God and the authority of his Messiah, for the accuser of our comrades has been thrown down, who accuses them day and night before our God. *But they have conquered him by the blood of the Lamb and by the word of their testimony, for they did not cling to life even in the face of death.* Rejoice then, you heavens and those who dwell in them! But woe to the earth and the sea, for the devil has come down to you with great wrath, because he knows that his time is short! (Emphasis mine)

It turns out that it is not Michael and his angels' violent power that enables them to conquer the dragon and his angels. The dragon is conquered by the suffering death of the Lamb, the testimony of the faithful witnesses, and their own willingness to die. In the language of the Gospels, it was the cross of Christ and the willingness of Christ's followers to take up their own cross that enabled them to defeat the lying dragon and his angels. In Walter Wink's language, the suffering of the slaughtered Lamb conquers the lies of the dragon and redeems those who have been wrongly accused. Again, what appears to be a Lion-like exercise of power in the book of Revelation confounds us by being a profound proclamation that the slaughtered Lamb has conquered.

The book of Revelation is filled with enigmatic symbolism and images of violence. But, in the end it is a hymn of praise to the Lion/Lamb who has conquered by his suffering death. In utter protest to the deceptive Myth of Redemptive Violence that had been propagated by the Roman Empire, the book of Revelation offered an alternative way of seeing the world, through the Myth of Redemptive Suffering.

Conclusion

The whole scenario of Jesus coming again as an Ahnold-like, clawed-up Lion who makes the world safe for God by means of destructive violence is simply wrong. It is a depiction of Christ's return that pretends to be based on apocalyptic biblical texts, particularly texts from the book of Revelation. But, if we allow John himself to demonstrate for us how to read the book of Revelation—by participating in the startling turn of events when the Lion *is* the Lamb in Revelation 5—then the common distinction between Jesus' first Lamb-like coming and his second Lion-like coming dissolves. Jesus is not bipolar, his Lamb-like personality is not a vanishing part of the overall Jesus story, and the Lion is not Jesus' evil twin Ahnold who is returning to undo all of the work that Jesus did. Neither is Jesus' return the kind of peace-through-violence that is often depicted in Left Behind Theology.

The book of Revelation depicts Jesus as the slaughtered Lamb who has already conquered, and by whose suffering the lies of the empire and its minions are likewise conquered. The violent imagery is real, to be sure, but violence in the book of Revelation is the real context, the reality of life that John's community was facing. John himself was in exile for his testimony to Christ. The point of Revelation is neither a form of escapism from the violent context of the world nor engagement in the violent conflict in order to overcome it with greater violence. The point of Revelation is to rejoice, to live in utter defiance of the arrogance and violence of the empire, because the slaughtered Lamb has already conquered.

Certainly the violence of the book of Revelation is inescapable. But violence is not the point; redemption is. Perhaps that is why it is a book filled with doxologies and songs of praise, none of which questions the outcome of the encounter between the Christian witness and the violent resistance of the world. As Walter Wink delightfully says, "The Book of Revelation may be gory, surrealistic, unnerving, even terrifying. But it contains not a single note of despair. . . . We have here no sober pilgrims grimly ascending the mount of tears, but singers enjoying the struggle because it confirms their freedom. Even in the midst of conflict, suffering, or imprisonment, suddenly a hymn pierces the gloom, the heavenly hosts thunder in a mighty chorus, and our hearts grow lighter."[6]

6. Ibid., 321.

Conclusion

Left Behind and Loving It

THROUGHOUT THIS BOOK, I have tried to offer a number of reading strategies for how we can faithfully read the scary apocalyptic texts from the Bible. From a sheer literary perspective, I have tried to show how ill-fitting it is to read poetic texts literally. It is not—as many Left Behind Theologians argue—a sign of unbelief to question literal readings of apocalyptic texts. It is a way of taking apocalyptic texts seriously to read poetic texts poetically.

I have also tried to show that biblical writers often indicate to us how to read their writings. The voice changes in Daniel, the abrupt tense changes in Mark, the subtle changes between Luke's and Mark's versions of the Olivet Discourse, Matthew's concluding story of the confused sheep and goats at the final judgment, and Revelation's startling moment when the Lion *is* the Lamb—these are all deliberate and meaningful ways that the writers have self-consciously invited us to read their texts with comprehension. Most importantly, the differences among the biblical writers are just as much reflections of their faithfulness and their inspiration by God's Spirit as are their similarities.

Most of all, I have tried to demonstrate that apocalyptic texts in the Scriptures can be read as beautiful and courageous expressions of the God who is made known to us in Christ, particularly in the midst of utter tragedy. By reading apocalyptic texts *as* apocalyptic texts, one can embrace them faithfully, while not interpreting them literally. Because of that, we need not believe that we are living in the "last days" in a literal, temporal sense. We need not believe that God's love is on a timer that is perilously close to striking the final hour. We need not believe that the Scriptures teach anything like the so-called "rapture," whereby God's elect will be swept away from the earth while others are left behind to suffer God's wrath. We need not believe that Jesus' meek and mild personality is a vanishing point in the larger story of violence. We need not believe that God will ultimately overcome evil through violence. We need not believe these things because we can believe in the gospel that is made known explicitly in Jesus Christ, the Lion who *is* the Lamb, at the center of the scary apocalyptic texts.

When we read apocalyptic texts *as* apocalyptic texts, we can come to a more profound and ultimately more faithful understanding of what it means to be children of God. We can believe that God's steadfast love endures forever. We can believe that the manner of God's steadfast love is made known and made real most explicitly through the life, death, and resurrection of Jesus Christ. We can believe that the Day of Pentecost marks how God's own loving Spirit has been poured out into the church, in order that we might witness to God's steadfast love, even in the most difficult of times. We can believe that Christ comes to us, over and over again, incarnate among the needy, among victims of oppression, and wherever the story of redemptive suffering is embodied in our world. And we can believe that all of heaven joins in and rejoices in utter praise when God's people defy the lies of empire and embrace the Christian message.

When we embrace the message that "God's steadfast love endures forever," something powerful happens. We learn to sing in the face of tragedy. We learn to believe in the face of despair. We learn to witness in the face of death. Miraculously, it is precisely in these moments of weakness that God's strength in us is revealed most powerfully.

But, of course, the whole idea that God's strength is made perfect in our weakness (2 Corinthians 12:9) is the part of the Christian message that seems like utter foolishness to the world. For that reason, the struggle that is reflected in so many apocalyptic texts remains the true context of embracing the Christian message. Our message is not that we escape the world in order that God can overcome the violence of our world with a greater, holy violence. Our message is that in life or in death nothing can separate us from the love of God made known to us in Christ. For that reason, we consider it an honor to be "left behind" as witnesses to God's grace, come what may. Left behind, and loving it.